The Threshold of Democracy

"Reacting to the Past" Series

The THRESHOLD of DEMOCRACY

Athens in 403 B.C.

Third Edition

Mark C. Carnes
Barnard College
Columbia University

Josiah Ober
Princeton University

PEARSON
Longman

New York Boston San Francisco
London Toronto Sydney Tokyo Singapore Madrid
Mexico City Munich Paris Cape Town Hong Kong Montreal

BARNARD
REACTING TO THE PAST

Publisher: Priscilla McGeehon
Editorial Assistant: Stephanie Ricotta
Executive Marketing Manager: Sue Westmoreland
Managing Editor: Bob Ginsberg
Production Coordinator: Shafiena Ghani
Senior Cover Design Manager/Designer: Nancy Danahy
Cover Photo: © Getty Images, Inc.
Map Artist: Carlos Lantis
Senior Manufacturing Buyer: Alfred C. Dorsey
Printer and Binder: Phoenix Color Corporation
Cover Printer: Phoenix Color Corporation

Library of Congress Cataloging-in-Publication Data

CIP data is on file with the Library of Congress

Please visit our website at http://www.ablongman.com

ISBN 0-321-33303-9

8 9 10—PBT—09

Contents

Introduction: A Morning after the War

IN THE FOOTSTEPS OF THESEUS

In the dark you stumble. Your heart leaps. The Spartan ambush was on a night like this. Iron swords ripping into leather and flesh. A piercing scream. Arms frozen in terror. By the time you grabbed your sword they were gone. But you sensed a body at your feet. A warm, sticky fluid oozed through your sandals. It was a childhood friend, a member of your patrol. By morning, he was dead.

But that was then, back during the war. You force yourself to breathe. The war is over. The Spartans and their allies have gone home. You had tripped on a loose stone. The roads have probably not been repaired since the slaves ran off, when the Spartans occupied this part of Attica several years ago. With the city so poor, many citizens now do work suited only for slaves. Think of it! Free women serving as wet nurses, your own mother selling trifles in the Agora.

You check your bearings: Castor and Pollux remain high in the sky, but Taurus has begun to slide toward the western horizon. Taurus, the bull! Was the constellation named after the Minotaur, the monster that dwelt beneath the palace of King Minos of Crete and devoured the Athenian children in ancient times? That was when Crete was a great power and Athens a mere vassal, obliged each year to send a boatload of children for sacrifice. Throughout your lifetime, though, it's been the other way round: Athens has collected annual tribute payments from other states, not of children but of silver. Will Athens now become a vassal of Sparta?

Back then, in Athens's time of need, Theseus had emerged to slay the Minotaur. Then he brought the many tribes of Attica together so that they became one: the *demos*—the people—of Athens. You remember, too, that Theseus had walked along the very road on which you now tread. Perhaps it was where you stumbled that Theseus, then sixteen, had come upon the half-beast who murdered wayfarers for the fun of it. But Theseus was half-god, and he threw the beast over a cliff, the first of his many deeds to rid Athens of its enemies. But that was long, long ago, when the gods mingled with human flesh and begat people of divine proportions. Nowadays people are smaller, and the gods pay them less heed. Perhaps that's why things have gone all wrong.

The sun smolders beyond the eastern horizon, and a faint haze extinguishes the stars. Darkness loosens its grip on earth, and you can see the outline of the hills and valleys of Attica. The fields should soon be coming to life. It is the season of *Boedromion*—"the time to harvest olives," as Hesiod had written so many generations ago. Last night after dinner you had unrolled your volume of his treatise on farming and showed it to your cousins and uncles, but they teased you. "Better to study things as they are, and not the symbols of them," they said. But as you described his advice, they listened. "Leave the fields fallow every other year" you read aloud, and saw that they were nodding in agreement. "Be sure to have a sharp-toothed dog to keep away thieves"—as you intoned Hesiod's words you stared at the shaggy mutt by the fire. Everyone laughed. "No matter," your uncle replied. "The thieves won't bother **this** year. Nothing left to steal.

Spartans have burned the wheat and barley fields between here and Athens, and they've ripped up most of the grape vines and fig trees. Even the sacred olive trees."

His words weighed upon you. They still do. More than ever, Athens needs good leadership. You walk more quickly. Today you intend to speak at the Pnyx [pih-NIX]. There may be no more heroes like Theseus, but Theseus bequeathed as his legacy the Assembly, a means for Athenian citizens to come together and solve their problems. You recall the first time you spoke. The herald's voice had boomed, "Those who wish to speak should now come forward." When you stood up, your friends doubled over in laughter. To their amazement you walked down to the rostrum and took place in the line of speakers. You looked up and for a time could not find your friends. When you finally spotted them, they were open mouthed.

But you were prepared. For years you had observed closely what others had said during the Assembly, and how they said it. You had taken notes on who prevailed at the law courts and why, and which actors won the theatre contests. You studied their words and mannerisms. You bought books on rhetoric, preferring especially the intricate strategies of Gorgias: break your argument into little pieces, he had written, and list the objections to each. Then refute them, one by one. He was a brilliant rhetorician, all the more impressive for being a foreigner.

And you had listened to Androcles, a good teacher despite his perverse insistence that you refrain from analogies. "A weasel's way of arguing," he insisted.

The restlessness of the crowd unnerved the speaker at the rostrum before you, and he stopped in mid-sentence. There were some jeers, and he ended his talk hastily, without any peroration at all. You took a deep breath. The Herald nodded to you. You strode to the rostrum and gazed up at the sea of faces. A lout jeered, "Wait 'til you've grown a beard, dearie," and others near him laughed. Androcles's words came to you: "Pause, but not too long, lest the hecklers fill the void." You plunged ahead and concentrated on your list of points, one for each finger of your left hand, another trick. At first your words tumbled out, but then you recalled Androcles's advice: "Speak slowly and clearly. Find a friendly face, or imagine one, and speak to it." As you slowed down, your words began to flow. Finally, you unclenched the final finger, delivered the peroration with suitable emphasis, and blinked. It was over. The crowd had been silent. "Well done!" several shouted.

As you climbed the steps, your knees trembled and you couldn't find your row. Strangers reached out to clap you on the back and grab your hand. Your heart soared. They had **listened**! You now recalled that several people near the front, the ones who customarily copied out the speeches of the best orators, were scribbling away during yours. After the Assembly was dismissed, someone expressed amazement that, in a crowd of 6,000, they could hear you from the top row.

But that, too, was before the war. Athens cannot live in the past any more, nor can you.

AT THE DIPYLON GATE

The eastern sky is brightening, but the sun has not yet cleared the twin peaks of Mount Parnassus. Within Athens, thousands are awakening. They, too, will soon be hurrying to the Pnyx, carrying bags of figs and bread dipped in olive oil to tide them through the afternoon. The Assembly promises to be a long one. Usually the city-people get the best seats. You hasten along, but the road has become clogged with farmers, all rushing toward the Dipylon Gate. You know that similar throngs are streaming through the other dozen or so gates of Athens. The road from Piraeus will be choked with perhaps a thousand citizens, mostly oarsmen who used to be paid by the state to row the *triremes* [TRI-REEMs], the immense warships that had for decades defended Athens and ensured its superiority throughout the Aegean. But now the *triremes* are gone, destroyed, or seized by the Spartans. How will the sailors make a living now?

A shaft of light strikes the Parthenon, atop the Acropolis, the citadel of Athens. For nearly a century it was invulnerable. In the time of Theseus, the wild warrior-women— the Amazons—had swept down from the Black Sea and nearly forced their way up and into the fortress. But they failed. Many decades ago, the Persian horde under King Xerxes [ZERK-ZEES] had seized the Acropolis for a time. Your great grandfather was among those who served in the navy that destroyed the Persian fleet in the Gulf of Salamis later that year [480 B.C.]. It was after more Athenian victories two decades later that Pericles [PEAR-a-KLEEZ] had called for construction of the Parthenon [begun 447 B.C.] as a gift of thanks to Athena. Many said that the temple, though dedicated to a goddess, was really a monument to Pericles and his democratic experiment.

Until just last week, Spartan soldiers had camped in the shade of the Parthenon and had stored weapons within the temple. Some say that if Pericles had not died so early in the war Athens would not have been defeated. Like so many Athenians, he was taken by the Great Plague—that was twenty-six years ago [429 B.C.], when you were still a child. That you survived was something of a miracle, or so your relatives claimed. Pericles had erred, many said, in abandoning the countryside to the Spartans and crowding within the gates of Athens. Pericles thought the people of Attica would be secure behind its Long Walls, a fortification that stretched for miles to Piraeus, protecting both cities and creating a safe corridor between. No one would go hungry because grain ships from the Black Sea and Egypt could unload at Piraeus and transport food and other necessities by cart through the protected corridor to Athens. The Athenian navy, with hundreds of *triremes*, was invincible; it would ensure the safe arrival of grain ships. Everyone knew that. But the city became overcrowded, with tens of thousands of people inhabiting rude huts along the inside of the Long Walls. Then came the plague, and many thousands died, more than could be buried properly.

Athens had not surrendered then, and the war continued, interrupted by a few brief truces. Nor did it surrender ten years ago, after the disaster in Sicily, when the 50,000-man Athenian invasion force was lost. The better part of an entire generation of the young men of Athens never returned from the other side of the world. Sparta set up permanent camps beyond the walls, and some 20,000 Athenian slaves fled into the countryside. Yet even then Sparta could not breach the walls of Athens. Many said that proved the wisdom of Pericles's strategy.

Until last year [405 B.C.]. Then the Athenian generals committed the horrible blunder at Aegispotami. They had allowed the Spartan navy to capture or destroy nearly 100 *triremes*, many of them pulled up on the beach. Those Athenian sailors who surrendered were butchered. With the Spartan navy free to blockade Piraeus, the grain ships could not get through. The Spartan army then tightened its siege outside the Long Walls. Last year the people of Athens and Piraeus went without food. For months they held out. Better starve, most reasoned, than be butchered by Spartans. Spartan mercy, the saying went, was an oxymoron. (The Athenians recalled their own lack of forbearance when, years earlier, the Assembly ordered the execution of all the men of Melos and the enslavement of their women and children; Melos's crime was having allied with Sparta.)

Last spring, with many dying from hunger, Athens at last surrendered. And Spartan troops marched through the Dipylon Gate ahead and set up camp in the Acropolis, from which vantage point they could keep an eye on everyone.

You notice that the crowd has funneled into a bottleneck at the gate. You see that some avoid it simply by climbing over the rubble of the ancient walls, great squares of cut stone. You take the short-cut, too, hurrying past the boulders where Spartan soldiers had stood, stiffly and silently, supervising the work as half-starved Athenian laborers dismantled the walls. Young girls had played the flute while soldiers from Thebes and Corinth—Sparta's allies—wore garlands of flowers. They also danced and sang. Never again, they said, would the Athenians impose their will on other Greeks. But you wonder: will those states now impose theirs on Athens?

AT THE AGORA

You arrive at the Agora, the lifeblood of Athens where all roads converge. Vendors are setting up stands and merchants are opening their shops. Many of the merchants are metics, foreign born residents who pay a fee to live in Athens. There are fewer than in the past, and some of the shops are gone. You had expected as much. You check the sun. You will be at the Pnyx within twenty minutes—plenty of time—and you cannot resist taking a stroll. You walk across the race track toward the monument to the Ten Tribal Heroes. A group has crowded around, but only a single message is posted: "Assembly Today."

After the Spartans had occupied Athens and destroyed its Long Walls, a similar notice had been posted. You had gotten up early that day, too. Critias was the first to speak—and the last. He explained that democracy had failed Athens. He added that the Spartans had no desire to destroy the Athenian people, but only to rid Athens of its democracy. He called it a pestilential form of government that endangered all Greece. The Spartans, he added, were aggrieved that the Athenian democrats attempted to install democratic governments throughout the Aegean, and even in Ionia and Sicily. The Spartans did not want to kill Athenians; they wanted merely to be rid of its democracy. Thus the survival of Athens required the elimination of the democratic system that had been imposed on it during the time of Pericles. The people of Athens would be spared, he declared, if they followed his counsel.

He called on appointment of thirty prominent citizens—he read their names—who would determine the ancient "constitution" of Athens. They would temporarily rule the city.

Eventually, Critias added, the Council of Thirty would be guided by an Assembly limited to 3,000 substantial citizens—those who would do what was best for the city without looking for state handouts or the fees paid to rowers on *triremes*. Some shouted objections, but Critias gestured toward the Spartan troops standing attention and ringed along the top of the Pnyx, spears at the ready. "If we do not do as I propose," he added, "Athens will be turned into a pasture." This brought more shouts, but most people could not take their eyes off the Spartans. The man next to you muttered. "It's a done deal." Critias's plan was endorsed. The Council of Thirty would govern Athens; the democracy was dead.

THRASYBULUS AND THE CIVIL WAR [404-403 B.C.]

You pause as you walk past the law courts. That's where the evil began. The evening after Critias's takeover, he ordered the arrest of several prominent democrats. They were quickly tried for treason and executed. "The city must be purged of unjust men," Critias declared, and "the rest of the citizens must be inclined to virtue and justice." It began as an attack on some of the more foolish and Radical Democrats whose policies had led to the humiliation of Athens. But Critias then hired a police force of 300 young men who carried whips, seized weapons from democrats, and otherwise intimidated them. The thugs singled out metics for harassment and arrest, especially those who were rich and possessed large fortunes. Then still more democrats were arrested. Whenever an arrest turned into a riot, Critias's soldiers ran to the Acropolis to fetch the Spartans. Many democrats fled Athens. A few vowed to destroy Critias and the Thirty Tyrants, as they were now called.

Thrasybulus [Thrah-SIHB-yoo-lus] was leader of the democratic insurgents. A successful naval commander, he came to notice eight years ago. This was after the failure of the Sicilian expedition. Then Athens had frantically built a new fleet and sent it to intimidate wayward tributary states. When the navy intervened in a civil war between oligarchs and democrats on the island of Samos, an oligarchical faction in Athens staged a coup and overthrew the democracy here. At the time [411 B.C.], Thrasybulus took charge of the sailors in Samos, delivered a rousing speech, and persuaded them help restore the democracy in Athens. When the fleet arrived at Piraeus, the coup collapsed and Thrasybulus was among those credited with saving democracy. (Thrasybulus later became a *trierarch* and was involved in a notable naval victory against the Spartan fleet [Arginusae, 406 B.C.], but was subsequently censured for failing to rescue sailors whose ships had sunk.)

Last winter Thrasybulus, after escaping from the Thirty, rounded up support from democratic leaders throughout Greece. Then he set up camp in a hill fort at Phyle, north of Athens, and declared war on the Thirty Tyrants. Several hundred democrats joined his band. He put out word that metics and even slaves who fought with him would win rights as citizens of Athens. Several hundred metics enlisted in his army, as did perhaps a hundred slaves. Within several weeks he had an army of nearly 750.

The Thirty cracked down even harder on the remaining democrats in Athens. In all, about 1,500 were executed, most without trials. Then Critias and his supporters, backed by the Spartan garrison, marched out to Phyle to crush Thrasybulus. But Thrasybulus attacked first, caught Critias by surprise, and inflicted heavy casualties. That night the

Thirty set up camp in the field, but it snowed and continued throughout the next day. The Spartans abandoned their attack and trudged back to Athens. Thrasybulus's astonishing victory drew more to his camp. A few nights later his army slipped around Athens and into Piraeus, where he took a strong position on a hill within the city. The Thirty attacked the next day, backed by 700 Spartans, but again were thrown back. Over 100 Spartans were killed, and Critias lay dead, too. The democrats controlled Piraeus.

There were more battles last year. For a time Thrasybulus and his ragtag army seized the initiative. But his troops were ill prepared; most carried shields made of wicker, not bronze or iron. The civil war became stalemated. Lysander, commander of the Spartans in Athens, proved clever as well as resourceful. But then something mysterious happened. No one has explained it to your satisfaction. Pausanias, one of the two Spartan kings, brought an army to Athens and decided to negotiate an end to the civil war. Perhaps he worried that Lysander was becoming too powerful. Perhaps he was appalled by the butchery of the Thirty, whose horrors brought no luster to Sparta. Perhaps he worried that Thebes was becoming a greater menace than vanquished Athens. Or perhaps he wearied of the lengthening list of Spartan casualties in what was a war between Athenian factions. In any case, Pausanias met with Thrasybulus, and with the moderate Athenian Oligarchs—those who disapproved of the Thirty. The two sides—democrats and Oligarchs—agreed to compose their differences and establish a government based on the ancient constitution of Athens. (What that meant was anyone's guess.) Then Pausanias withdrew the Spartan garrison. This was just last week. Within hours, the Thirty Tyrants were gone, too, having fled. Yesterday, Thrasybulus and his men marched triumphantly back into Athens. And word was posted that the Assembly meetings would resume. Today.

AT THE COBBLER'S SHOP: THE RADICAL DEMOCRATS

As you hasten through the Agora, you spot Thrasybulus at the cobbler's shop. His arm remains bandaged from the wound he received at Piraeus. You wonder if he killed Critias by his own hand.

You notice that Thrasybulus is animatedly conversing with Anytus, wealthy owner of a tannery. Huddled with them are several metics; one slave is also talking and gesturing. You know a number of slaves, as well as metics, joined democrats in Piraeus and fought bravely against the Thirty Tyrants. They had acted as if they were citizens; doubtless Thrasybulus intends to propose that such as these be given actual citizenship.

One of the Radicals—a friend-- calls you over. You gesture to the swords and wicker shields that have been piled next to the stacks of leather. What, you ask, will happen at the Assembly today? "We shall see," he says. "The forces of oligarchy are tenacious. We all thought they had been finished off eight years ago, when we put down the oligarchical coup [of 411 B.C]. But they came back, and with bloody vengeance. Now people again say that the Thirty are gone and that oligarchy is disgraced for good. But these tyrants have been around for ages. Even a century ago. The Peisistratid tyrants. They had to be killed off. Same with these tyrants, too. The only time you can deal with them is when they're dead. We must root out all of the enemies of democracy once and for all."

But what of Sparta?

"Why did Pausanias leave? he asks. "Not because the Spartans tired of Critias's butchery, I can tell you that! No. They returned to Sparta because Thrasybulus sent so many Spartan soldiers on the long, last journey below. As I see it, it doesn't make much difference whether we fight oligarchs in Spartan armor or Athenian oligarchs wearing embroidered cloaks in the Assembly. They're all of a piece. And all must be defeated, once and for all. The first step is to add more democrats, to replace those who have been killed off so methodically these past few months. We need to bring in some more people with nerve, proven friends of our ancestral democracy!"

He offers some barley cakes, but you gesture toward the Pnyx and stand. He tugs at your tunic: "We're trying something new, you see? The kings of Persia and Sparta, the tyrants of Syracuse and Carthage, the oligarchs of Corinth—the whole world hates and fears democracy. But we know it works. It gives people a say in their destiny, so they work and fight harder. When the Persians herded their huge army into Greece, driving them forward with whips and spears, they were amazed that the Athenian soldiers came charging on the run, ready to die for their state. A few months ago, when we ambushed the Spartans at Phyle, screaming with fury, some of them ran, piss dripping down their legs. Spartans! I tell you, democracy is the way of the future. But it won't just happen. Some imagine that the merits of democracy are so obvious that it cannot be defeated. They are wrong. Democracy will prevail only when the enemies of democracy have been extirpated. We're in for a fight."

His words send a shiver down your spine. As you leave, somewhat hastily, you beg his forgiveness.

AT THE MONEYLENDERS' TABLES: THE SOCRATIC SCHOOL

Just beyond the bankers' tables where he always hangs out, you spot Socrates, a notably ugly and ill-kempt old man. He is famous—even infamous—for his startling views and irrepressible wit. He says that the Athenian people are like sheep; that they are easily swayed by powerful orators, whether in the Assembly, the law courts, or the theatre; that they make fools of themselves in pondering—collectively!—complicated issues of jurisprudence or affairs of diplomacy and warfare; that they are more concerned with pilfering drachmas from the public treasury than with ascertaining justice and promoting virtue; that they do not think much, or often, or well. The more he indicts the people and institutions of Athens, the more his students applaud him, or so some of his critics maintain.

You recall that Socrates was the subject of the first play you ever saw—*Clouds*. It was by Aristophanes, in the new style—a comedy. Why, you wonder, did Aristophanes and comedy become all the rage during the nearly three decades Athens was continually at war? In *Clouds,* Aristophanes portrayed Socrates as keeper of a "think-shop" who floats among the clouds: "Never could I have discerned matters celestial, if I did not mingle my intellect with its kindred air." One Strepsiades, beleaguered by debts, approaches Socrates to learn "Wrong Logic" so as to confuse and evade his creditors. In a favorite scene, Socrates inquires as to Strepsiades's aptitude for logic. Socrates asks,

"Is your memory good?

Strepsiades: "It all depends. Good if someone owes me; if I owe someone, alas, it is very bad."

Socrates: "Have you a gift for speaking?"

Strepsiades: "For speaking, no. For cheating, yes."

Socrates: "What do you do if someone hits you?"

Strepsiades: "I wait a bit and get witnesses. Then I file suit."

Like everyone else, you had laughed. But now Socrates is regarded differently. You notice the grim expressions of the young men gathered about him by the tables. You spot Plato and Xenophon, young men of good families who have always been among Socrates's gabby gathering. They look worried. There were whispers about Socrates and Critias even when the Tyrant held absolute power. Now that Critias is dead and gone, many remark that Critias had been among Socrates's most faithful students. Socrates had also taught Alcibiades, who had betrayed Athens eleven years ago (although, during the oligarchical coup of 411 B.C., Alcibiades had helped Thrasybulus). Some ask whether Socrates had taught Critias and Alcibiades the Wrong Logic that culminated in the crimes of the Thirty.

Socrates apparently envisions a society where philosophers—like him and his students?—serve as rulers, while eschewing the pleasures of wealth and power. The "guardians," as they would be called, are to lead simple, chaste lives, dedicated solely to the welfare of everyone else. Even women, if adjudged intellectually superior, are to be among the ruling elite of this utopia. There are to be no Assembly meetings or *dikasteria* (public law courts), which Socrates says encourage the ignorant to discuss matters beyond their comprehension. Nor will there be publicly-sponsored plays, which teach people the arts of manipulation and encourage falseness. (And where people go to laugh at philosophers like himself!) The ultimate goal of the Socrates and his supporters is to purify thought and in so doing to help thinkers arrive at a deeper understanding of ultimate truths. Words must be defined with precision, and ideas must fit together according to the rules of logic, devoid of the human passions and cravings that impair the operation of reason. Thought must be reflective, and not intuitive. His is an ambitious notion.

Socrates's students now take their leave and head toward the Pnyx, carrying no weapons but their wits. Socrates himself holds back. This most garrulous of Athenians refuses to take part in meetings of the Assembly, or so they say. But sometimes you thought you had seen him there, holding back in the shadows.

AT THE BARBER'S SHOP: THE OLIGARCHS

As you cross near the race track, you spot several prominent Oligarchs huddled inside a barbershop. Some are wealthy—you recognize one whose father owns an enormous vineyard near Phyle which was worked, before the war, by scores of slaves. But most Oligarchs are simple farming folk much like your relatives last night. One voice rises above the others. "We don't need—Athens doesn't need—any more tyrants, like Critias and his thugs." Several nod in agreement. "Our city should be ruled by a large group of the best men, those who care about Athens and know what is best for it." More nods. "That's what we stand for. We spit on Critias and those of his ilk. But the fact that he was evil does not prove that his enemies were blameless, or that their views are good ones." A man next to the speaker lifts a goblet of wine in a toast, and the others do likewise; they lower their voices, and then burst out in laughter.

Now the others join in. Almost to a man, they denounce Pericles's strategy for the war, which allowed enemy soldiers to pour into Attica unmolested while Athenian farmers, most of them well-trained and well-armed as foot soldiers (*hoplites*) and everyone else had scampered to safety behind the Long Walls. Occasionally, *hoplite* patrols or a handful of countrymen sneaked out and ambushed small Spartan detachments. "Oh, yes," you say, "but sometimes they got us, too." "But it was Pericles who insisted that we give up battles on land." And so it was, as everyone knows, that Athenians fought with their best weapons (the formidable *triremes*) and on terrain (the sea!) where they were invulnerable. Thus while the Spartans were despoiling the fields of Attica, Athenian sailors and *hoplites* were boarding *triremes* and conducting lightning raids along the Peloponnesian coast and elsewhere. Whatever the merits of this type of warfare, the cost to the Athenian farmers and landholders was staggering. In addition to the destruction of their homes and fields, the periodic disruptions of the countryside—the Spartans would usually attack during harvest season—encouraged thousands of slaves to run away. Scores of moneylenders were ruined, and trade collapsed.

During the war, too, land owners, large and small, had paid the heaviest taxes. The richest citizens had to build and maintain *triremes*. It was an honor, of course, but also an unspeakably expensive obligation. Most of the state revenue, moreover, went to pay the rowers of the *triremes*—the *thetes*, the poorer citizens of Athens and Piraeus who reported for military service with no weapons save their oars. Your uncles complained that when such men could not find work, they crowded into the Assembly and voted for new expeditions or demanded that they be paid merely for showing up at the Assembly or the law courts. Pericles obliged them, and they became his staunchest supporters; and those who owned land became his fiercest foes.

The supporters of oligarchy eye the wine bowl, but the steward, on signal from the owner of the shop, begins to gather up the drinking implements. To bring the session to an end, he declares that patriotism, virtue, and self-restraint are the basic principles of oligarchy. Critias and his ilk conformed to none of these principles. "We want order, stability, and prosperity. People must acknowledge that society is fragile. Its needs must take precedence over the desires of the individual. Society works smoothly, if at all, only when everyone accepts limits on their own behavior. Pericles's great fault was hubris: he imagined that all Athenians could become whatever they desired. That conceit is at odds with the hard realities of the world, foremost among them the defects of human nature." The others nod. "We can wish that every shoemaker can become a statesman," he adds, "but that sort of thinking is why we lost the war."

"It's time for a change," another declares, thumping his fist upon the table, his face red from exertion—or perhaps the wine.

"Well, yes and no," the owner interrupts. "Plenty will say that our humiliation is reason to try anything. Let metics who don't even speak Greek become citizens! Or slaves, who would as soon cut our throats as their meat. Others will propose that we let wooly-headed sophists decide how to conduct future wars. But you and I know that time is the best test of all ideas, and that traditional beliefs have endured for good reason. Those who sail into the unknown may imagine that they will find boundless treasure; probably, though, their bones will end up on the floor of the ocean. In this time of crisis, Athenians must exercise discipline—of their polity, and of themselves. Though they may wish to eat to their full, they must accept that gluttony is a vice; though they may wish to drink wine all day and seduce their neighbor's wife"—he frowns at the red-faced friend, and the others burst into laughter—"they must learn to work and be self-controlled; though they may want to live to a ripe old age, they must be willing to give their life for their country. We must do so, too. Men, we must go."

As you leave the colonnade, you notice a pile of weapons stacked outside the Stoa, watched over by stewards. The Oligarchs and Democrats had agreed yesterday not to bring their weapons to the Pnyx, but you wonder.

AT THE POTTER'S SHOP: THE MODERATE DEMOCRATS

You leave, too, but can't resist looking in at the pottery shop, a bee-hive of activity; the workers are an interesting mix. Some are free, and some are skilled slaves, most of whom are paid wages and can keep a portion for themselves. Some were imported from truly savage regions, such as Thrace and Scythia. Some rise rapidly. Some become managers. A few become rich. Women slaves are almost always assigned to look after houses, or be weavers, maids, nurses, and prostitutes.

You know the owner of the shop, a leader of the Moderate Democrats. When you ask why he didn't flee Athens and join Thrasybulus and the Exiles, he explains that he thought it better to stay to help his city as best he could.

His friends long for the days of Pericles, and hope that another such as he will emerge during the current crisis. Had Pericles lived, one says, Athens would never have lost to Sparta. Another declares that he was the great leader of that or any age. Another adds that his sentences were like chiseled marble. To prove his point, he declaims the Funeral Oration [430 B.C.]: "Our political system does not compete with institutions which are elsewhere in force. We do not copy our neighbors, but try to be an example. Our administration favors the many instead of the few: this is why it is called a democracy"—and on and on he goes.

Pericles's genius, another declares, was leadership. "He knew how to make Athenians put aside their differences and work for a common goal. Like at the Olympics. Athenians learned to cooperate, whether singing in choral competitions, rowing a *trireme*, or acting in a play." "When Athenians work together," he adds, "they are invincible. We lost to Sparta because madmen on both sides drove a wedge through the polity and broke it apart."

The Moderates say that Athens must return to the golden age such as Pericles inaugurated a half century ago. They want to see the Assembly filled with earnest citizens, debating and talking and thinking and educating themselves and the world. They want to elevate the common people to serve even as presidents and magistrates. Athens has become great because even the humblest citizens contribute to its glory. The Moderates long to restore the Athenian empire, to build more glorious temples and government buildings, to hold more festivals with more theatrical productions, and to again establish Athens as the center of the civilized world.

Their vision, too, is an impressive one.

TO THE PNYX

The voice of the Herald booms out, calling the citizens to order. Soon the *peristarchos* will sacrifice a pig, as was done at the time of Theseus, to ensure that the gods bestow favor on the deliberations. Now you run, and your thoughts race ahead, too.

What you say and do at this Assembly session, and the ones in the months ahead, will affect your life, and surely the lives of your children and grandchildren. The survival of Athens depends on you. Perhaps some descendent of Thucydides will write down what you do and preserve it for posterity. The fate of civilization, in **your** hands! You chuckle at the thought. But then a shiver runs down your spine. It may be true.

The Game: Basics

WHERE SET

This game is set in Athens in Autumn of 403 B. C. Each class session will be take place either in the Pnyx, an open-air amphitheater where the Assembly is held, or in one of the nine law courts, where trials are held. Some classes may include both an Assembly session and a trial.

YOUR ROLE IN THE ASSEMBLY, INCLUDING SPECIAL JOBS AS ASSEMBLY PRESIDENT, ARCHON, OR HERALD

You are an Athenian citizen. (Some versions of the game include a non-citizen metic, a foreign-born resident of Athens.) You are necessarily a man: women are denied permission to attend the Assembly or the law courts. You are over thirty years of age (a requirement to serve as a juror in the law courts). You are accorded all of the rights of a citizen of Athens. In sessions of the Assembly and in the law courts, you are free to speak on whatever issues you wish. You can propose laws, impose taxes, erect buildings, and even recommend public sponsorship of a particular play. The Assembly decides all such matters by a majority vote of citizens present.

The Assembly sessions are held about forty times a year, though they had been suspended under the Thirty. The Pnyx seats about half of Athens' 16,000 citizens. (Some Athenian citizens live in colonies established in Asia Minor, Macedonia, or remote islands in the Mediterranean; some are too busy tending their farms in rural Attica to attend sessions of the Assembly; a few do not care about politics.)

You are among the 6-8,000 Athenian citizens who show up at every meeting of the Assembly. At these meetings, the citizens of Athens make virtually all decisions about how Athens is to be governed: whether to modify the laws or go to war; whether to build new aqueducts or temples; which plays to produce at public expense, etc. You care intensely about Athens and how it is governed.

Furthermore, you have a substantial political reputation and rhetorical powers. People listen to what you say and follow your advice; and members of your large extended phyle—voting area, roughly synonymous with your clan—look to you for guidance. This is reflected in the fact that at all meetings of the Assembly, you control—at least for now—500 votes. When an issue is to be decided in the Assembly, you have the power, in effect, to cast 500 votes as you wish. It so happens that the other citizens [in the classroom] each controls 500 votes as well.

The notion that the citizenry should collectively decide public business extends to the legal system, where any citizen can initiate a public or private lawsuit and the matter will be decided at a *dikasterion*, a law court. You are among the 6,000 or so citizens who show up each month on trial day, where citizens are randomly assigned to one of the nine law courts. The jury for most courts consists of 500 citizens plus the magistrate. When you speak, you persuade: you control [as do the other citizen-leaders seated around you] 40 votes [or 50, depending on class size] of jury members.

Like any good Athenian citizen, you do not hesitate to seek office. Nearly all leadership positions in the Athenian government are determined by a random lottery of all citizens. This, too, is an affirmation of the democratic ethos that no citizen possesses intrinsically more merit than any other, that the best "ruler" of Athens is the collective judgment of a majority of its citizens. Thus all citizens interested in any government position place a ball with their name on it into a machine; after all the balls have been submitted, the machine spits out, through a random process, a single ball and that person gets the job. It is assumed that you have entered your name for all possible positions, of which three types are to be chosen prior to the first Assembly meeting:

> **President of the Assembly**, who presides over a single meeting of the Assembly and sets the agenda in advance of the meeting;

> **Archon** [ARK-ahn], one of several magistrates, each of whom presides over one of several law courts; and

> **Herald**, who opens meetings of the Assembly, delivers a prayer, and arranges for the ritual sacrifice of a pig.

There is one exception: if you are a metic, you are not a citizen and are thus ineligible for all of these positions, unless the law excluding metics from citizenship is modified.

The Main Factions

SOCIAL DIVISIONS

Now, as in the past, Athenian citizens will decide the nature of the new government through their participation in the Assembly and their work as juries in the law courts. But decades of foreign and civil wars have fractured the polity perhaps as never before. Most Athenians belong to one of four political factions: the Radical Democrats, the Moderate Democrats, the Oligarchs, and the Socratics. Other citizens are unaligned, at least at present. [They are identified here as "indeterminates".] Often, but not always, the political factions are linked to social/economic classes. The poor generally support the Democrats; and the wealthy, the Oligarchs.

CLASS DIVISIONS

The political divisions to some extent mirror class divisions. All citizens are expected, at least until they attain old age (their forties or fifties), to provide military service; citizenship and military service have always been linked. But there are two main types of military service: those citizens rich enough to own their own armor (bronze or iron body armor, an iron shield, sword, and spear) serve as *hoplites*, soldiers who are trained to fight on land in a tightly-coordinated unit called a *phalanx*.) Those who cannot afford armor belong to the *thetes* [THEH-TIS] class; they report for duty in the port of Piraeus, carrying an oar, and become rowers of the *triremes*, the formidable three-tiered warships. (A third type of military service, numerically fewer than either the *hoplites* or *thetes*, are the *knights*, armored warriors who fight on horses in the cavalry. Knights must report to their cavalry unit with their armor, horse and a servant to tend both. The *knights* are the elite branch of the military.)

The very richest Athenians are also expected to serve as *trierarchs*, the owners, builders, and even commanders of a *trireme*. When the Assembly votes for war, it will commonly call on its richest citizens to become *trierarchs*. This is a signal honor; it is also an obligation the rich cannot evade.

The *hoplites*, who almost always are property owners, generally support the Oligarchical views on government and politics. The *thetes* usually look to the Democrats, Radical and Moderate, for guidance (and for financial support). But one's class does not always dictate one's position on any particular political issue. It is wrong to assume that a wealthy person is opposed to democracy, or that a poor one favors it. People do not always think as their pocketbook dictates. Some of the most prominent democratic leaders are wealthy; and some of the most enthusiastic Oligarchs are not.

METICS AND SLAVES

Another division concerns the metics, some 20,000 foreign-born people who work in Athens, chiefly as artisans and shopkeepers, and who perform many essential services. Thousands of metics have served as mercenary soldiers and sailors, a requirement for foreign born men living in Athens. Some metics are very wealthy, and this generates some tension between struggling Athenian citizens and the prosperous (and, some say, the enterprising) metics.

The experiences of slaves vary enormously. Slaves in the silver mines to the north work in 12-hour shifts, day and night, and are subjected to almost bestial conditions. At the other extreme, some slaves in Athens acquire skills and live quite independently, assigning part of their wages to their owner. Most property-owning farmers are expected to own at least one slave to help with household tasks. Some slaves are acquired by war; others are bred as slaves, children of slave parents.

If the Assembly votes to give citizenship rights to metics, that "indeterminate" representing the metics may then cast "his" 500 votes in the Assembly, and also serve as a *dikaste* in law courts.

NEARLY EQUAL SIZE OF FACTIONS

It might seem that the landless *thetes* would greatly outnumber the property-owning *hoplites*. By this way of reckoning, one would then assume that the democratic factions would greatly outnumber the "conservative" Oligarchs and Socratics. Until fairly recently, they did. But nowadays the factions are fairly evenly balanced. This is chiefly due to the demographic consequences of the Peloponnesian war.

The war, lasting twenty-seven years, resulted in the deaths of thousands of Athenian citizens. But the losses were not apportioned equally among the two branches of military service. Because of the Periclean military strategy, the *hoplites* for the most part manned the Long Walls, protecting Athens and Piraeus from the Spartan army. But the Athenian navy (and its tens of thousands of *thetes*) ventured on innumerable raids and dangerous missions. Three decades of war sent hundreds of *triremes* to the bottom of the Aegean, resulting in the deaths of nearly 11,000 *thetes* (oarsmen); far fewer *hoplites* died in battle. Late in the war Athens was reduced to hiring mercenaries and metics to serve as *thetes*. Thus at present the total number of *hoplite*-citizens is about 9,250; and the total number of *thetes*-citizens is about 8,000. What this means, of course, is that the property-owning *hoplites* outnumber the *thetes*, although the economic depression of the past year has thrown many of the farmer-*hoplites* into penury. It is fair to assume that the Democratic and Oligarchical factions are nearly equal in size.

Here's another way of looking at the demographics. Today—in 403 B.C.--nearly 2/3 of all Athenian citizens own land. Some of the plots, to be sure, are small; others may be heavily encumbered with debt. But most landowners will tend to side with the political faction that seeks to restrict the vote to those who own real property: land. (The Thirty Tyrants had promised to relinquish political authority to The Three Thousand—roughly, those Athenians who owned significant landholdings; their failure to deliver on this promise contributed to their downfall.)

[The factions are probably apportioned as follows. If your class is larger than 16 or 17, or smaller than 14, you may have a different allocation of factions.]

FACTION	# of Faction Leaders	Representing # Citizens	Column for notes
Radical Democrats	THREE, including Thrasybulus	1,500	
Moderate Democrats	THREE	1,500	
Oligarchs	THREE	1,500	
Socratics	THREE	1,500	
TOTAL	TWELVE	6,000	

ADVISORY: JOINING WITH OTHER FACTIONS

Radical Democrats will find it advantageous to join forces with Moderate Democrats, and Oligarchs with Socratics. But you should remember that the objectives of each group are by no means identical. There may be issues where Radical democrats will vote with Socratics, etc. For example, the Moderate Democrats endorse the Reconciliation Agreement; the Radical Democrats **oppose** it. Similarly, the Moderate Democrats and the Oligarchs generally wish to avoid social experimentation, while the Radical Democrats and Socratics are generally in favor of revolutionary changes in the structure of society.

Proceedings of the Assembly

PRESIDENT OF THE ASSEMBLY

The President of the Assembly for the Day (chosen by lot) will preside over one day's session of the Assembly. All Presidents of the Assembly will be chosen at the outset of the game, and for a specific session.

Each President has considerable latitude to "preside" over the session as he sees fit, though he is expected to exhibit basic standards of fairness. The President is free, however, to take an active and even partisan part in the sessions over which he presides. The President should announce at the beginning of his session how he intends to proceed. He may impose time limits, though some free discussion should be encouraged. There is one limitation to the powers of the President, as follows:

> **PODIUM RULE:** Students, if they wish, can speak while seated. But it is important that every student, at least once in the Athens game but preferably more often, go to the podium to make a more formal statement or speech. Also, and this is important, students who find that they are not being recognized by the President of the Assembly owe it to themselves, their faction, the instructor, and the class as a whole, to approach the podium. With certain exceptions, enumerated below, students have an absolute right to stand at the podium to address the Assembly or the *Dikasterion*. The President is expected, at some reasonable point, to call upon the person at the podium. If one person is already waiting at the podium, others may join a line behind him to speak. The Gamemaster [i.e., supervising faculty member] will remind the President of the need to allow those at the podium to speak; if the President continues to ignores those at the podium, the instructor will remove the President and name another person to replace him.

CREATION OF LAWS

During Assembly sessions, any citizen may propose a law, decree, or action. All proposed laws should be submitted in writing to the President of the Assembly, and must bear the name of at least one citizen, or more, as author(s).

This is a requirement of Athenian law: all laws include the name of the author(s). If it happens that the law has harmful consequences, then the authors of the law can be held responsible and brought to judgment by the courts. If any proposed law is approved by a majority of those voting in the Assembly, it becomes a law immediately and possesses the force of law. All approved laws will be engraved in stone [i.e., taped to the blackboard, or posted to a class web site.] (Because laws must be chiseled in stone, brevity is a special virtue for prospective legislators.)

The consequences of any particular law may require some interpretive guidance by the Gamemaster. If the **Assembly** passes any law whose consequences are unclear, then the Gamemaster will eventually make a determination on how any law affects the course of

The Threshold of Democracy

the game. If, for example, the Assembly passes a law ordering all Athenian citizens to begin rebuilding the walls of Athens, one can assume that some citizens will do as commanded. But that does not ensure that the walls will go up rapidly. If opposition to the law was pronounced, and if some prominent leaders call for the law to be disobeyed, the walls may not go up so quickly. Similarly, if the Assembly votes to go on a naval expedition to coerce tributary states to make tribute payments to Athens, that expedition will be sent. Whether the expedition will **succeed** depends on the will of the Athenian sailors and soldiers (as well as that of possible enemies), the number of men and ships committed for the expedition, and the vicissitudes of wind, tide, and war. The Gamemaster will indicate the outcome of the expedition after the final session of the game. Issues that include matters of chance may include die rolls, the odds of which will be determined by the Gamemaster. The Gamemaster may also be obliged to invent such rules as make sense or seem otherwise desirable.

Voting shall be conducted by voice vote, or show of hands, with decisions determined by majority vote. The Herald will count the votes, as verified by the Gamemaster. The Gamemaster may post the vote totals on the blackboard or website.

HERALD OF THE DAY

The first person to speak at a full Assembly session is the Herald. The Herald's job is to ensure that the Assembly deliberations win the favor of the gods. The Herald will also count the votes of the Assembly, a tally that must be verified by the Gamemaster.

Traditionally, the Herald begins by presiding over the sacrifice of a pig. The Herald may perform that task herself or select someone to serve as the *Peristarchos* (pig sacrificer). The *Peristarchos* must wait until the citizens have settled in the Pnyx. Then the *Peristarchos* is to sacrifice a pig and drag it around the Pnyx, purifying the proceedings with its blood. Then the Herald is to declaim a brief prayer, or perhaps read an appropriate passage from a classic text.

[Advisory: There is no point in undertaking historical research to find exactly how the pig sacrifice was performed. The ancient texts don't reveal very much, such as the nature of the prayer. What we know about the herald and *peristarchos* comes mostly from a speech delivered in one legal case (Dinarchus: Speech 2), the text of which has survived: in the speech, the prosecutor accused the defendant of giving a speech in the Assembly whose purpose was to mislead the Athenian people; the defendant had done so, the prosecutor alleged, because he had taken a bribe. His crime was worse, the prosecutor argued, because in addition to deceiving the Athenian people, he had also offended the gods, because the Herald had, at the outset of the proceedings, invoked the gods to chastise those who "misled" or "deceived" the Athenian people. So, any herald/*peristarchos* is pretty much free to create whatever sort of ritual and prayer he wishes.] Clever Heralds may use the prayer to advance their rhetorical or political objectives. Or the Herald may wish to read a (not too long) passage from some classic text, or offer a prayer or a curse. Here's a "self curse" that appears in Homer's ***The Odyssey***.

[Odysseus, who had been away from home for many years and returns in disguise as a beggar, encounters a former servant and tells him that Odysseus is not dead. The servant is skeptical. Odysseus responds: "I see that even with my oath I have not won thee, nor find credence with thee. But come now, let us make a covenant; and we will each one have for witnesses the gods above, who hold Olympus. If thy lord [Odysseus] shall return to this house, put on me a mantle and doublet for raiment, and send me on my way to Dulichium, whither I had a desire to go. But if thy lord return not according to my word, set thy thralls upon me, and cast me down from a mighty rock, that another beggar in his turn may beware of deceiving."

And here is a pig sacrifice from *The Odyssey*:

"Bring the best of the swine, that I may sacrifice it for a guest of mine from a far land. . . . Therewithal he cleft logs with the pitiless axe, and the others brought in a well-fatted boar of five years old; and they set him by the hearth nor did the swineherd forget the deathless gods, for he was of an understanding heart. But for a beginning of sacrifice he cast bristles from the head of the white-tusked boar upon the fire, and prayed to all the gods that wise Odysseus might return to his own house. Then he stood erect, and smote the boar with a billet of oak which he had left in the cleaving, and the boar yielded up his life. Then they cut the throat and singed the carcass and quickly cut it up, and the swineherd took a first portion from all the limbs, and laid the raw flesh on the rich fat. And some pieces he cast into the fire after sprinkling them with bruised barley-meal, and they cut the rest up small, and pierced it, and spitted and roasted it carefully, and drew it all off from the spits, and put the whole mess together on trenchers. Then the swineherd stood up to carve, for well he knew what was fair, and he cut up the whole and divided it into seven portions. One, when he had prayed, he set aside for the nymphs and for Hermes son of Maia, and the rest he distributed to each. And he gave Odysseus the portion of honor, the long back of the white-tusked boar, and the soul of his lord rejoiced..."

Here is another prayer from *The Odyssey*, with the speaker's arms raised to the gods:

"Nymphs of the well-water, daughters of Zeus, if ever Odysseus burned on your altars pieces of the thighs of rams or kids, in their covering of rich fat, fulfill for me this wish:--oh that he, even he, may come home, and that some god may bring him!"

AGENDA ITEMS FOR THE ASSEMBLY

The first class will begin at the Pnyx as a session of the Assembly. The agenda for that class is fixed: **the Reconciliation Agreement.** (The President can propose an additional agenda item, too, though it must be discussed only after the debate and vote on the Reconciliation Agreement.) The Reconciliation Agreement agenda will seek to decide whether the Assembly should pass a law ("Reconciliation Agreement") granting amnesty to those who may have abetted the Thirty Tyrants. The law would also prohibit Athenians from filing lawsuits or even bringing to public notice the "past wrongs" of those who supported the Thirty Tyrants or somehow promoted their cause.

Other agenda topics (up to two/session) are as follows, though others not on this list may be proposed:

Leadership Selection: How should magistrates and those charged with executing the decisions of the Assembly be chosen?

Extent of Electorate: Who possesses the right to participate in the Assembly and the law courts as a citizen?

Social welfare for citizens: What actions, if any, should the state take to redistribute wealth, through taxation, from property owners to those without it?

Restoration of the Athenian empire: Should Athens remilitarize and send expeditions to force other city states to resume tribute payments to Athens?

Education of Young: What should the young be taught and by whom?

Socrates: Does he pose a threat to Athens by "corrupting" the minds of the young? By undermining Athenian culture and traditions? By ridiculing democracy and the people of Athens? Should he be silenced?

Maintenance of Core Cultural Traditions. Should fundamental Athenian religious beliefs and cultural values (apart from those listed above) be changed in a radical fashion? The following provide illustrations of what constitutes Core Cultural Traditions:

> Belief in, or at least public sacrifices on behalf of, the multiple gods of whom Zeus was the leader;

> Maintenance of slavery;

> Retention of a right to private property; and

> Retention of existing practices of courtship between men and boys, and men and women.

Laws that substantially modify any of the above or similar Athenian cultural practices will constitute an assault on these "core cultural traditions."

The agenda for the first session will include "The Reconciliation Agreement" (below) and perhaps a second topic chosen by the President.

STRATEGY ADVISORY: ON PRESIDENTS AND AGENDAS

If you belong to a faction, your side should outline in advance which Assembly presidents belong to your faction, or to a faction with which your team will likely form an alliance. Your faction should advise "its" presidents on the choice and timing of the preferred topics. Be mindful, too, that in the event of a major trial (i.e., of Socrates), one or two presidential sessions will be eliminated or abbreviated.

Proceedings of the *Dikasteria* (Law Courts)

INTRODUCTION

Athens democratizes its trials. To ensure fairness, and to ensure that the collective will of the Athenian citizenry is represented, each jury for a *dikasterion* consists of 500 citizens. All citizens of Athens over thirty are encouraged to serve as jurors in trials; all receive pay of 3 obols (1/2 drachma) for each trial day of service. (The normal daily wage for a worker was 6 obols, or 1 drachma.) On trial day, when as many as nine separate *dikasteria* might be held, each citizen puts a ball with his name on it into a machine, which randomly distributes potential jurors to different *dikasteria*. All jurors are then given a chit, indicating the name and location of the *dikasterion* to which they have been assigned. They then report for duty and submit the chit, which is necessary to ensure payment for their service as juror. As a good citizen, you will show up on trial days and will likely be assigned to a *dikasterion*. In the event of a trial, you will take part in the deliberations of the *dikasterion*, as juror, or perhaps as plaintiff or defendant. All decisions of the *dikasterion* are made by majority vote.

All trials are presided over by a magistrate (archon), himself randomly chosen at the outset.

TRIAL ADVISORY: HOW TO INITIATE A TRIAL

If you wish to charge any person (Athenian citizen or otherwise, present in Athens or not) with any offense, you should approach one of the archons. (The names of the archons are public knowledge; ask the Gamemaster if you forget their names.) If any one of the archons agrees that your case has sufficient merit to proceed with a trial, then that archon will request from the Gamemaster permission to schedule a trial. You will be notified if and when the trial has been scheduled. If one archon declines your request for a trial, you can approach any or all of the others. If no archon will accept your case, then it is dead.

If the Gamemaster schedules a trial, the person making the charge will function as the lead prosecutor. The prosecutor may invite others may join in this task.

LAWS AND LEGAL PRECEDENTS

Neither the prosecutor(s) nor the archon is **obliged** to cite a specific law or legal precedent that the defendant has presumably violated. The trial itself functions as a means of setting laws. For example, a Prosecutor could charge another person with the "crime" of eating figs during Assembly sessions, though no such statute seems to have existed in ancient Athens. If the *dikasterion* convicts someone of chewing gum, then all Athenians would know that chewing gum is violation of Athenian norms, and thus Athenian law. In short, Athenian citizens, acting as jury, set laws through their decisions. The Athenians equate the *dikasterion* with the people because, with 500 jurors, it represents a statistically significant sampling of the citizenry. The Assembly can also pass laws.

The archon will preside over the trial, setting procedural rules. The Athenian people expect that archons will behave in a fair and reasonable manner; those who fail to do so run the risk of being censured on the expiration of their term. The defendant may speak for himself or ask others to assist in this capacity. If Socrates is placed on trial, however, he will not speak in his own defense.

There is one legal distinction worth considering. Athenian law distinguished between offenses against the polis (the state) and against other private citizens. Both types of offenses were adjudicated by a *dikasterion*. But the nature of punishment differed. An offense against a private citizen required that the fine be paid to the victim of the crime; an offense against the state required that the fine be paid to the state. If Person X borrowed money from Person Y and failed to pay it back, Person X would likely be fined, with the payment going to Person Y. If, however, Person X hit Person Y with a rock, that would be viewed as a crime against the state because it threatened public order. Person X, if convicted, would make a payment to the Athenian treasury. It is significant that verbal attacks against persons were regarded as crimes against the state because they, like a physical assault, imperiled public order. The archon, in indicating that a trial is to go forward, should indicate whether it is of a public or private character.

SCHEDULING A TRIAL

If the Gamemaster agrees to a trial, the Gamemaster must schedule it by taking away some time from an Assembly session. In the event of a trial of Socrates, one or even two Assembly sessions will be truncated or eliminated. That time will then be used for the trial.

In most cases, a defendant will be given advance notice of the trial so as to prepare a defense. In some cases, that may not prove possible. A trial of a private character may be as brief as fifteen minutes and require little development.

SELECTION OF THE JURY

In Athens, each *dikasterion* consisted of 500 citizens who comprise the jury and hear the case; the 500 jurors were chosen randomly from the entire citizenry. For game purposes, all leaders (students), including the magistrate, will constitute the jury; each Leader will control 40 votes [or, perhaps, 50]. A vote of 7 to 5 will actually be 280 to 200. *Warning: Assembly leaders who have been penalized for non-participation may lose their ability to cast votes in the dikasterion.*

RENDERING THE VERDICT: VOTING BY MARBLES (OR SOME EQUIVALENT)

At the end of the trial, the Gamemaster will distribute marbles (or some other tangible marker) to each Leader (student), one type of marble to denote innocence, another guilt (each marble represents 40 [or 50] votes in the *dikasterion*). The Gamemaster will then place two urns on the table, hidden behind a screen. One urn represents the student's vote on guilt or innocence, the other urn is for the "discarded" marble. To vote, each leader will secretly deposit the marble indicating her vote.

However, to replicate the random character of jury selection in ancient Athens, the Gamemaster will not count ALL of the votes, only the first 12 marbles to spill out of the urn (fewer, for a class of less than 16 students, more, for a class of over 19 students) These will indicate the final vote. The Gamemaster will not disclose the color of the "uncounted" votes.

SETTING A PUNISHMENT

If someone is adjudged guilty, then the prosecutor will initiate a second phase of the trial to determine the penalty. The procedures here will be similar to the initial trial, though shorter in duration. The prosecutor(s) will propose a penalty, and the defenders will speak against it, and then there will be open discussion of the matter. [In fact, Athenian law courts did not allow open discussion in the penalty phase; this has been included to compensate for the brevity of the class, compared to the day-long trials.]

PUNISHMENT FOR FRIVOLOUS PROSECUTIONS

Athenian law included a provision to prevent what might be termed "frivolous" prosecutions. It provided that if a prosecutor failed to persuade at least 20% of the jurors to vote for "conviction," the prosecutor would be subject to loss of political rights. Thus, for the purposes of the game, if the Prosecutors fail to persuade 20% of the jurors to vote for conviction, then the Prosecutor(s) will automatically lose all of her votes in subsequent Assembly and *dikasteria*. Similarly, in this event, too, that archon will be publicly censured for allowing an unworthy prosecution to go forward. (If the archon is censured by a majority vote of the Assembly, that student will lose 20% of his voting followers.)

TRIAL OF SOCRATES: SPECIAL PROCEDURES

If an archon agrees, any citizen can call for a trial of Socrates. In that event, there are several special rules:

> Schedule: The trial will last nearly two full sessions, as scheduled by the Gamemaster. This will necessitate the eradication, or sharp reduction, of one or probably two Assembly sessions: the Gamemaster will likely schedule a Trial of Socrates in a way that allows a week for preparation; the Gamemaster will try to eliminate Assembly sessions (or abbreviate them) in a way that is fair; and the time allotted for prosecution and defense presentations and rebuttals will be greatly expanded, and set by the Gamemaster.

> Evidence: The evidentiary core of the sessions for a trial of Socrates consists of: Plato's *Republic*, the documentary materials in the introductory packet, the profiles of the indeterminates, and also any other historical materials before 403

B.C. (For example, chapters from Xenophon's *Hellenica* or Thucydides's histories.)

Socrates himself will not speak in his defense: he shall rely on others to do so.

TRIAL OF SOCRATES: HISTORICAL CONTEXT

Socrates is an important figure to several of the factions of this game. Those most concerned are the Radical Democrats and the Socratics. The Radical Democrats view him as a dangerous enemy because he tutored Critias and some other of the Thirty Tyrants, and because his most scathing criticisms are directed at democracy; the Socratic faction draws its inspiration from both the beliefs of Socrates (generally antidemocratic, to be sure) and from the power of his mind. The Moderate Democrats and the Oligarchs are less concerned over the fate of Socrates.

Historical Advisory: Here is what happened historically. In 399 B. C. Socrates, a citizen of Athens, was indicted as a "public offender" who 1) failed to recognize the gods of the state and instead introduced his own "demoniacal beings" and 2) corrupted the youth of Athens. The trial was held before a *dikasterion*, of 501 citizens. By a margin of sixty votes, he was pronounced guilty. His subsequent "apology" ("if you kill such a one as I am, you will injure yourselves more than you will injure me") sealed his fate. By a larger margin than before, the jury condemned him to death. Socrates disdained the opportunity to escape, and thus ensured his martyrdom. He drank the hemlock and the rest, as they say, is history. The account of what he said in his defense can be found in the Perseus Project website (www.perseus.tufts.edu) in the Platonic dialogues, especially the *Apology, Crito,* and *Phaedo,* as well as Xenophon's *Apology.*

> *Note: Although those dialogues cannot be cited within the context of the game because they occur after it, the arguments may prove to be useful to defenders of Socrates. Moreover, the words of Socrates as cited in The Republic, CAN be cited, verbatim, as trial evidence. That's largely because Plato, one of his disciples, witnessed the events and wrote many important books based on what he had seen of Socrates prior to 399 B.C.. Whether the "Socrates" described in The Republic was historically valid or substantially the creation of Plato and others is unclear. For the purposes of the game, we shall assume that Plato's rendering of Socrates in The Republic and other works is accurate.*

Nowadays [Modern World] people still read and care about Socrates—or, rather, Plato-as-Socrates—because his relentless examination of the workings of the mind constitutes an enduring expression of the power of reason and the glory of man. Plato has also been important because his anti-democratic worldview, which troubled the citizens of Athens nearly two and a half millennia ago, has stood as a powerful challenge to democrats ever since. Clear resonance of the arguments aired in Athens in 403 B.C. can be heard in debates throughout the world today.

Victory Objectives

STRATEGY ADVISORY: HOW TO INTERPRET THE CHART

You "win" if, at the end of the game, your faction has achieved a high point total. It is possible, and even likely, that two allied factions will win: say, Democrats (Radical and Moderate); or conservatives (Oligarchs and Socratics). But in a close game, exactly who is prevailing is subjective. To assist the Gamemaster in making this decision, and to give you some guidance on how your faction is doing, you should consult the following "Victory Objectives Chart."

The "victory objectives chart" is an attempt to advise students on the relative value to each faction of different decisions of the Assembly and *dikasteria*. The best strategy is to advance your side's political philosophy, especially to the indeterminates, and to hinder those whose political vision differs from your own. Generally, two factions will win, and two factions will not. "Winning" for the indeterminates is more complicated; it usually involves some ongoing discussion with the Gamemaster.

Sometimes it is possible to win a game with blind luck or clever political maneuvering. But the best approach by far is to win over as many indeterminates as possible. What this entails is making "your" vision of society persuasive and coherent. If you focus on certain objectives, you may yourself lose sight of your larger purposes. This will make it impossible to persuade others to come to your side. Each faction has a fairly coherent and expansive **vision** of what it wants Athens to become. As a Leader in a faction, you should aspire to make that vision a reality—at least in the classroom. You should strive to realize the vision, not to just to accumulate favorable adjectives; the former is, indisputably, a better means of accomplishing the latter.

Warning: The following chart provides some general sense of how the various factions are faring during the game. This chart provides, necessarily, only an **approximation** of the implications of any action. Partly that's because adjectives are not really quantifiable; they are approximations also because the actions depend on the actual phrasing and details of the various decisions. The Gamemaster determines the "winners" only at the end of the game. If you attain one of your objectives early in the game but lose it at the end, only the final result will matter.

VICTORY OBJECTIVES CHART (APPROXIMATIONS)

OUTCOME	Radical Dems.	Moderate Dems.	Oligarchs	Socratics
GOVERNMENT AGENCY				
Assembly makes all decisions (as at beginning)	+3	+6	0	0
Government positions selected by lot (as at beg.)	+6	+4	0	0
Council (appointed by Assembly) sets policies	-1	-1	+3	+5
ELECTORATE				
Voters, as at present, do not need to own property	+3	+6	0	0
Electorate limited to those who own land or equivalent property	-2	-2	+6	+3
Electorate broadened to include slaves (or metics) who fought against Thirty Tyrants	+2	0	-2	0
Electorate limited to those who have attended special schools or otherwise shown intellectual merit	-4	-2	+3	+6
SOCIAL WELFARE				
All citizens who attend Assembly to be paid	+6	+3	-1	-3
RECONCILIATION AGREEMENT				
Passed: illegal to "remember the wrong" of Thirty Tyrants or their sympathizers, no lawsuits allowed against any faction of that era	-3	+4	+4	+2
RESTORATION OF ATHENIAN EMPIRE				
Assembly votes for property tax to rebuild long walls between Athens and Piraeus	+2	_+1	-1	0
Assembly orders construction of fleet of *triremes*; orders collection of special property taxes to pay *thetes* for 6-month campaign	+3	+2	-2	-1
Assembly orders military expedition to collect tribute from one of 5 zones: Ionian, Hellespontine, Thrace, Cyclades, Black Sea	+4	+3	-3	-1
Military expedition succeeds, tribute paid: higher number for expedition against major tribute states in Ionia, lower for expeditions against minor tribute states in nearby islands (See map, "Tribute Districts of Athenian Empire")	+4 to +8	+2 to +5	0 to+2	-3 to -5
Assembly does not vote to build *triremes* or mount any tribute expeditions	-4	-2	+6	+2
Military expedition results in Athenian defeat	-6	-3 .	-3	+2
TRIAL OF SOCRATES				
Socrates placed on trial, convicted	+9	+6	0	-6
. . . and executed	+6	-2	-2	0* (depends)
Socrates placed on trial, acquitted	0	0	+6	+9
Socrates not placed on trial	-3	0	+4	(depends)
MAINTENANCE OF CORE CULTURAL TRADITIONS				
Revolutionary or radical changes in basic religious or family values (? = depends on nature of change) Education	+?	-?	3(-?)	+?
. . . Public education to teach democratic values to youth	+3	+1	-3	-2
. . . Private education by family/sophists	-3	-1	+3	-1
. . . Publicly funded education for intellectual elite regardless of class or gender	-2	0	-3	+3

Indeterminates

Not every citizen of Athens is a member of a partisan faction, and not all members of a faction agree on every issue. Some Athenians are, at least at the outset of the proceedings, undecided on the various issues confronting the city-state. And some Athenians care more about matters whose relevance to the factional disputes is unclear. These citizens are known as Indeterminates. Because the four main factions are of nearly equal size, they will try to persuade Indeterminates to support their positions. Athens's political fate largely depends on what the indeterminates, acting individually, decide to do.

An indeterminate role is something of a contradiction in terms. The "victory objectives" of the Indeterminates are incomplete, imprecise, or undisclosed. Each student will be given the persona of a particular type of person who lived in Athens in the late fifth century B.C. Each Indeterminate is responsible to the Gamemaster for making his actions—his written and oral work and, of course, his positions on various issues—plausible within the parameters of his assigned persona. And yet the role is indeterminate in the sense that each indeterminate is expected to express some measure of her own character. This is an insoluble issue, insofar as none of us can fully determine to what extent our beliefs represent our independent, core sense of self and to what extent we have learned them from our society and culture.

The Indeterminates, though often undecided, still function as Leaders: they command 500 votes in the Assembly, and forty [or 50] votes in the *Dikasteria*. They will participate in government, holding positions as President of the Day (in the Assembly), Archons, or Heralds.

The possible "Indeterminate Leaders" are selected from among the following. How many indeterminates are included in your game depends on the number of students; the allocation of indeterminate roles is mostly random. You may not be able to tell which "indeterminate leader" is associated with which "public biography" that is included in the packet (See Appendix A).

INDETERMINATE	Number of Leaders	Representing # Citizens
Fishmonger	ONE	500
Retired Sailor	ONE	500
Impoverished Farmer	ONE	500
Merchant son	ONE	500
Rich Athlete	ONE	500
Bearded artisan	ONE	500
Middling Farmer	ONE	500
Carpenter	ONE	500
Metic	ONE	No Citizens (but the metic leader speaks for many in the large metic community)
? (added by instructor?)		
TOTAL IN GAME	(3-9, depending on class size)	

In a class of sixteen students, for example, only four of the indeterminate roles will be used (these being selected randomly). In addition to the public biography, available to everyone, each indeterminate will have a private "role" assignment, which will provide more information about "himself," some of which will not be publicly disclosed.

Early in the game, indeterminates may prefer to explore particular questions that concern them in formulating a fuller worldview; they may or may not choose to take stands on various issues raised in the Assembly. But at some point during the game, perhaps during Session 4 or thereabouts, each indeterminate will meet privately with the Gamemaster to describe how "he" is beginning to conceptualize "his" persona. The Gamemaster will advise whether the persona is "credible" (i.e., consistent with the cultural context and biographical circumstances outlined in the "public biography" and the private "role sheet".) Any indeterminate whose adoptive "persona" fails to meet this plausibility test will "lose."

In addition to representing particular aspects of Athenian society, some indeterminates represent historical factors that impart further verisimilitude to the game.

General Advice on Strategy: Papers and Oral Presentations

It is unlikely that any single faction, or even alliance of two factions, will have enough votes to prevail either in the proceedings of the full Assembly, or in a *dikasterion* (court). To prevail in such settings, you will doubtless need the support of a majority of the indeterminates. You do so by **persuading** them to vote with you as often as possible. You must frame arguments in your writing and your spoken presentations in ways that make sense to them. You may tailor your arguments to fit their special circumstances. You should read carefully all of the Indeterminate Biographies in the Game Packet. To make things easier, you may wish to ask the indeterminates which particular indeterminate person they "represent." They are under no obligation to answer. Perhaps you should invite them to meetings of your faction. (Remember an overarching rule of all games: No one may violate the U.S. Constitution, the rules or this college or university, or the laws of the state or municipality in which it is located.)

In this game and all others, you will find it easier to frame your arguments by seeing how your historical counterparts did so. They spent much of their life finding persuasive arguments; there's no reason why you shouldn't learn from them. Read through the "Pertinent Documents" section of the Game Packet. All defenses of democracy, for example, begin with Pericles's famous funeral oration, given to commemorate the dead early in the Peloponnesian war. Democrats should read it for advice on what they might say; anti-democrats should read it for clues on what they will have to attack. So, too, Oligarchs should read Alcibiades speech at Sparta for his indictment of democracy (an "acknowledged folly"); and democrats should be aware of Alcibiades' his criticisms. Plato's *Republic* (Part IX, or, in some versions, [Books VIII and IX]) provides a useful (though not unpartisan) account of the defects of democracy, oligarchy, tyranny, and "timarchy." Aristotle's *Politics*, Book 6, contains a useful discussion on how to ameliorate the weaknesses of democracy and oligarchy. There are many other materials; seek help from the Gamemaster.

Although the Internet is far inferior for most purposes to good research libraries, it is extremely convenient and useful for searching ancient texts, many of which have been placed on the Perseus Project website. If you would like to look through nearly all the extant writings of ancient Greek writers (Plato, Thucydides, Herodotus, Sophocles, Aristophanes, Aristotle, etc.), log into the Perseus project website at Tufts. If you wish to cite it in a paper, do so as follows: Gregory Crane (ed.), The Perseus Project, www.perseus.tufts.edu, March, 1997.

An important strategy issue concerns **focusing topics**. The issues that will surface in the Assembly (and *Dikasterion*) are difficult and complex. No one can be expected to master them all in a short time period; nor can any single paper or speech make a persuasive case on **more than one** issue. A student in the Socratic faction would grievously err if she were to write a five-page paper, and give an oral presentation, on: "Why the Socratic Republic is better than Democracy." The subject is far too big and complex. She would almost surely fail to make any point persuasively; and the paper would be unfocused. For her, a better rhetorical strategy (and one that would likely result in a better grade) would be on topics such as: "Why the Ignorant should not Vote," "A Plan for Educating Rulers: Finding the Best and Training them to Rule," or "Let's Put Executive Power into the Hands of a Governing Council," etc.

A corollary of the need to focus arguments is the fact that, to cover **all** of the issues, factions should carefully **subdivide their workload**. For example, one Radical Democrat Leader may wish to concentrate on the merits of equality, especially as they pertain to **Electorate** (who gets to vote); another Radical Democrat. on issues of **Government Agency** (why the Assembly should make most decisions, rather than, say, the Assembly Council); and another Radical Democrat, on the need for remilitarization of Athens. The success of each faction depends largely on how well it apportions work and oversees its execution. Keep in mind, too, that if your faction has three members (most do), then at least one member has to make a presentation at EVERY public session of the Assembly or, in the event of a trial, at the *dikasterion*.

When allocating the workload, keep two additional things in mind: first, issues will doubtless emerge that you have not anticipated. Make sure that you have an idea of who will be responsible to fill in the holes at the last minute; second, it is probable (but not inevitable) that one week (two whole sessions) will be devoted to a trial of Socrates. In preparing your initial papers and presentations, always be mindful of how those arguments can be adapted to function in a trial of Socrates. If, for example, you are Moderate Democrat and have assumed the task of speaking/writing in support of random selection of magistrates and leaders, you should be prepared to challenge the argument of Socrates [in *The Republic*] that justice is obtained when shoemakers make shoes, physicians tend to the ill, and rulers make political decisions and subjects obey them. [Random selection would have shoemakers sometimes making decisions about government.] By keeping in mind Socrates' argument in your early work, you would be prepared to show—in a trial of Socrates—exactly how it posed a danger to Athenian democracy.

All of this is by way of saying that everyone must have a fairly strong grasp on Plato's *Republic*, which contains [the game asserts] an accurate rendering of the views of

Socrates. These views will doubtless be raised by the Socratic faction, and perhaps by the Oligarchs; in any case, Socrates's views constitute a tremendously powerful (if maddeningly slippery) critique of democracy. By framing philosophical arguments on most issues in relation to Socrates's arguments, you will be well-prepared to address nearly any issue that surfaces during a trial.

Winning: Bonus

Some instructors may offer a grade bonus to the winning students' "class participation" component of their grade (assigned by the instructor). This underscores the point that, in life, one best advances one's personal goals by working effectively within a team.

As in life, too, winning is not necessarily a reflection of merit. One may play the game brilliantly and still not win; conversely, a lackluster performance may prevail. Sometimes, the accidents of chance—or fate—determine the outcome. The objectives of some roles are more difficult to attain than others. This is not fair; nor is life. The gods bestow their gifts unequally. Do your best; do not despair. If you don't win this game, you may win the next.

Special Rules

RETENTION OF LEADERSHIP POWERS

At the beginning of the game, each student/Leader controls 500 votes in the Assembly, and 40 or so votes in the *dikasterion*. This is in cognizance of the student/Leader's rhetorical abilities, which presumes that student/Leaders will speak effectively in class sessions. Students who are members of any of the four factions are expected to speak **at least** once each week in the Assembly or the *dikasterion*. Any faction member who **fails** to speak during either session of any week will lose 100 votes in all future Assembly ballots; a failure to speak for **two** weeks would result in a loss of 200 votes. (Failure to participate in class, of course, also affects one's class participation grade.) The instructor makes all decisions in such matters.

The Gamemaster will advise student/Leaders who are in danger of losing votes. To register a voice vote ("I vote 'yes'") or pose a simple question will not qualify as "speaking". Making a substantive comment while seated at the table **does** qualify as speaking, as does, of course, making a speech, or delivering an extended question at the podium. Recall: all students have the right to approach the podium so as to ensure their opportunity to speak. The Gamemaster will prod the Assembly President to ensure that everyone at the podium is called on, sooner or later.

DISQUALIFICATION FOR READING ALOUD. Reading aloud is rarely an effective rhetorical strategy. Often it is boring and unsuited to an impressive leader such as yourself. You are permitted to read aloud your **first** speech; but you should not read subsequent speeches. You are encouraged to consult 4 X 6 cards or notes.

Indeterminates are under no such obligation, at least through week 5, although participation is recommended. Indeterminates are encouraged, at the very least, to ask questions and seek clarification of confusing points.

Any student who loses 100 votes in the Assembly will also lose the ability to cast a proportionate number of votes in *dikasterion* as well.

ROLE OF GAMEMASTER, CONTACT WITH INSTRUCTOR

The Gamemaster's role is to do everything possible to make the game an intellectually broadening exploration of late Fifth Century (B.C.) Athenian society and thought. The game, accordingly, is complex. As the myriad elements of the game collide in innumerable permutations, chance will intervene in ways that the Gamemaster cannot anticipate. If the game careens wildly from historical plausibility, the Gamemaster may intervene, perhaps by modifying the rules or roles.

Most roles are difficult and challenging, as are the accompanying texts. Students should not hesitate to discuss their problems and confusion with the Gamemaster. If, by the third week, you have not spoken privately with the Gamemaster (or the instructor), or exchanged at least one e-mail, you are probably playing the game poorly. E-mail is often a good way to initiate queries, because the process of formulating a question in words helps clarify your thinking. The Gamemaster, in responding to such requests, will try to formulate a helpful response without taking into consideration the various other issues that may be swirling around.

That is: the Gamemaster knows far more than you do about the game, its permutations and complexities, and its evolving modifications. But in responding to particular queries, the Gamemaster will try to see the situation solely from the perspective of the questioner, without reference to what other players are doing or may likely do in the future. This is a way of saying that the Gamemaster will do her best to refrain from sharing your views and strategies with anyone else; conversely, you cannot assume that the Gamemaster will alert **you** to someone else's strategy or proposed initiatives.

STUDENT-INITIATED RULE MODIFICATIONS

Students may find that the constraints of the game (definition of roles, allocation of powers, descriptions of "victory objectives") are not consistent with their understanding of ancient Athens. Such students are encouraged to appeal to the Gamemaster for a change in the rules or the addition of new ones. Let's imagine, for example, that you support a military expedition to the former Hellespontine tribute district, and you believe that it cannot possibly fail [i.e., you want to argue that no die roll is necessary, or that its odds are much in your favor]. To that end, you may wish to conduct research on the subject and present it to the Instructor, perhaps as part of your written work for the game.

[In this instance, you would wish to consult Russell Meiggs, *The Athenian Empire* (1972).] The Gamemaster may or may not be persuaded by your brief; she may or may not change the rules. You may or may not be informed in advance of her decision. But it is fair to assume that the Gamemaster will appreciate thoughtful research.

OSTRACISM

One of the earliest democratic measures, perhaps dating from the revolution of Kleisthenes in 507 B.C., is ostracism. Once a year, the President of the Assembly calls on the citizens to vote on whether there will be an ostracism that year. If a majority votes in the affirmative, all of the citizens write the name of the person whom they wish to ostracize. The person whose name is included on the most ballots is then ostracized, or exiled from Athens for a period of ten years. Ostracism was largely abandoned by the Greeks after 418 B.C, but for the purposes of the game it is still a viable option. [In the game, no ostracism can be proposed **before** the 5th Assembly session; and there can only be one ostracism for any game. If there is a decision to go forward with an ostracism vote, the Gamemaster will distribute slips of paper to all members of the Assembly. Each will write the name of a person she proposes for ostracism. The person whose name appears on the most ballots will be ostracized. The Gamemaster will notify the President of the Assembly of the outcome; the ostracized student will presumably be banished from Athens, obviously incapable of voting on any measures before the Assembly or participating in any *dikasterion*. If she holds a position in the Athenian government, the replacement for that position will take her place.] *WARNING:* This is a powerful and unsettling weapon, used rarely by the Athenians. Those who **proposed** ostracism were sometimes the objects of the ostracism they initiated.

GRAPHE PARANOMON

This is another way to initiate a legal attack. All laws passed by the Assembly are chiseled into stone; the name of the person or persons proposing the law is also included. Someone can initiate a "graphe paranomon" by giving a speech denouncing the author of a law or decree that is contrary to existing laws in form or content. If a majority of the Assembly concurs, the law is annulled.

WARS OF TRIBUTE

Historical Narrative

In 478 B.C., after the Persians under Darius and Xerxes had twice mounted enormous invasions of Greece, Athens persuaded a handful of Greek city-states (Delos, Naxos, Thasos, Samos, Chios, Lesbos, etc.) to enter into a mutual defense pact (known as the Delian League) and to make annual payments of silver into a common defense fund, stored in Delos. Some small, impoverished cities paid several thousand drachmas; most city-states paid from 2 to 9 talents a year; the largest and wealthiest paid 40-50 talents. (A talent was a hunk of silver about the size of a human head.) Athens was always the most powerful state in the Delian League, but by the mid-fifth century, it dominated the League as never before. In 465 the island-state of Thasos refused to pay its 3 talents of tribute and withdrew from the League. The Athenian Assembly declared this action to be unacceptable. It dispatched the Athenian fleet to Thasos, destroyed the Thasos fleet, and then besieged the city of Thasos, which surrendered in 463. The walls of the city were dismantled, her silver mine and ports were transferred to Athenian ownership, and it was assessed a punitive annual tribute of 30 talents.

Within two decades, about 150 to 200 city-states paid annual assessments to Athens. Many of them bristled at the practice. Rebellions were frequent, and occasionally exploded into outright war; but most learned that it was wiser to pay than to suffer the might of the Athenian navy and the wrath of its citizenry. In 454 the silver reserve of the Delian League was transferred to Athens and stored in the vaults of the Acropolis. This marked the end of a mutual defense league and the beginning of the Athenian empire. By then, the annual payments totaled nearly 500 talents of silver. The total reserve was perhaps 8,000 to 10,000 talents. Pericles, the great Athenian orator, proposed using part of the reserve to build the Parthenon to honor the goddess Athena. This project, which commenced in 447, was the first of several construction projects which gave work to many of the poorer citizens of Athens.

One talent was sufficient to pay the salary (one drachma/day) of 170 citizen-rowers of a *trireme* for an entire month. An impressive 100-*trireme* expedition (20,000 men—about 40% of Athens available soldiers in 431) would expend 1,200 talents for six months. Few city-states could resist a force of such size; none could pay for that type of extended naval operation.

In 446 Sparta, alarmed by Athens's increasing power, sent an invasion force by land into Attica. That war sputtered out. By 431 B.C., when Pericles called upon Athens to go to war with Sparta, the reserve fund consisted of about 6,000 talents. This marked the beginning of the Peloponnesian War. It would last 27 years.

Advisory: How to Reclaim the Athenian Empire

This probably requires action of the Athenian Assembly. The easiest action would be for the Assembly to vote to rebuild the Long Walls, which the Spartan garrison dismantled less than a year ago. There is some risk that Sparta will become alarmed by this action and send its army to again crush Athens. On the other hand, Thebes to the west is growing more powerful, and Sparta may worry more about Thebes than an Athens that has been utterly humiliated. Rebuilding the walls is an essential first step for the resumption of the Athenian empire; otherwise, the citizens of Athens will be vulnerable to foreign attack while the Athenian navy is prowling for tribute.

The Assembly can vote to build a fleet of *triremes* and also fund the salary for rowers to serve for a 6-month expedition (this would be sufficient to ensure resumption of tribute payments) to any one of Athens's former tribute districts.

Finally, the Assembly can dispatch the fleet to any of the former tribute districts: The Assembly legislation should specify which district (s) are being visited:

Ionian District, Island District, Thraceward District, Hellespontine, and so on. Each of the Tribute Districts includes from 27 to 65 city-states that are charged to make tribute payments. Expeditions to Ionia and the Hellespont may unsettle the Persians; those southward toward the Island District may worry the Spartans. (See map of the tribute districts.)

After the final sessions of the *dikasteria* and Assembly have been held, the instructor will role a die to determine whether any military expedition succeeded. The greater the margin in the Assembly for war, the better the chances of Athenian victory. If Athens wins, then city-states in that district will likely resume tribute payments. Note that the wealthiest tributary states will likely be the most difficult to subdue. No one knows in advance the odds of success of any military venture, though wise leaders will do everything in their power to strengthen their armed forces before going to war.

While nearly all positions in the Athenian government were determined by lot, there was an important exception: every year, ten citizens were elected as generals (*strategoi*). The Assembly can remove generals, too. The Assembly may wish to name its generals and any other plans after a vote for a military expedition is announced. For example, the Assembly may need to make proposals for how to finance the expedition, which could include raising taxes for the rich, selling citizenship to the metics, confiscating temple treasures (that is, "borrowing from the gods"). See Xenophon's *Poroi*.

Classroom Schedule

The early sessions of the "Athens" game will consist of introductory lectures on ancient Greece and conventional analysis of Plato's *Republic*. This work is crucial to the game sessions for several reasons. *The Republic* constitutes a brilliant and enduring analysis of the weaknesses of democracy (and also, though less relentlessly, of oligarchy); nearly all antidemocratic thought borrows from some aspects of the arguments outlined here. *The Republic*, too, represents an ingenious attempt to develop an argument for social organization based on moral reasoning; to this point, most justifications of government were framed in terms of self or class interest. Finally, *The Republic* provides an early foundation for logic and rhetoric, the essential skills of philosophical inquiry.

After the roles are distributed, lots will be taken to determine who will serve as President of the Day for each Assembly session; as Herald for each Assembly session; and as one of three or four archons, for the duration of the game. (In all likelihood, only one or two archons will ever have cause to hear a trial.) The list and schedule of all positions will be posted on the class website, or distributed to the class in some other manner. Consult, too, the **Schedule of Action** for a session-by-session description.

CLASS 1: INTRODUCTORY MEETING OF CLASS

The Instructor will distribute the course syllabus and provide a brief introduction to Greek history in the fifth century B.C. (500-400 B.C.). The Instructor will also inform students as to where they can find the "Athens in 403" student game packets.

CLASS 2: GAME INTRODUCTION CONTINUED

Reading/Discussion of Plato's Republic (Books I-III)

The class will begin with a brief lecture on Plato's *Republic* and discussion of the following. Before class, students should read: the Game Packet (entire, carefully!) except Documents; read also the essay on the Peloponnesian War by Josiah Ober at the end of the booklet AND the following sections of Plato, *The Republic* (Penguin):

> Part I: Introduction;
> Part II: Preliminaries;
> Part III: Education: The First Stage

Questions to consider

Early in Book I, Plato/Socrates poses a difficult question: what does one mean by the term "justice"? One of his flock suggests that an instance of justice is manifested by paying one's debts; and another, giving a man his due (doing well by those who deserve it, and ill by those that do not). Socrates demolishes these arguments easily. Then Thrasymachus (threh-SIHM-ih-cus) argues that justice is a construct of those in power: "I say that justice is nothing other than the advantage of the stronger." A derivative maxim of this argument is, "Might makes right." How does Socrates argue that this view is unsound?

Socrates then leads the discussion along a meandering path with reference to ship captains, doctors, and veterinarians. What is his point in arguing, "Tell me, doesn't every craft differ from every other in having a different function"? Socrates concludes: "anyone who intends to practice his craft well never does or orders what is best for himself—at least not when he orders as his craft prescribes—but what is best for his subject." What is logical purpose of this argument? Does it have a political purpose as well?

Thrasymachus scores some points with the observation that shepherds take care of the sheep until they're ready to be slaughtered, hardly proof of the shepherd's "interest" in the sheep. How, and why, does Socrates refute this? What is the purpose of the famous analogy to thieves?

Beginning on (Part I [Book II], Ch. 4), Adeimantus and Glaucon restate the argument. "Those who practice justice do it unwillingly and because they lack the power to do injustice," Glaucon states. Justice is, for most people, a matter of convenience (they are afraid of getting caught) or adherence to traditions and rituals or a longing for rewards (i.e., getting into heaven). Glaucon concludes

his interesting hypothetical situation with: ". . . how is it possible for anyone of any power—whether of mind, wealth, body, or birth—to be willing to honor justice and not laugh aloud when he hears it praised?"
Socrates provides his answer in the Preliminaries. What does Socrates say and why?

What, to Socrates, is the origin of society? How does this relate to his preceding arguments? What is the connection to his argument and Athens evolution as a trading city-state? Why, in a discussion of justice, does Socrates discuss the quality of diet in his hypothetical city? Why mention that the people will not only have good food but fancy desserts, "consisting of some dessert, figs, and peas, and beans. . ."?

What is the relation of the "bigness" of societies to war and social instability? What is the logical justification for a specialized "guardian" (or ruler) class? Political justification?

What is the implication of the watchdog analogy (Part II [Book II], Ch. 3)?

In Part III, "Education: The First Stage," what **deductive proof** does Socrates use to argue that many myths about the gods are false? Why does Socrates, himself something of a gadfly in Athens, want to indoctrinate the young with particular stories and beliefs? ("Then our first business is to supervise the production of stories, and choose only those we think suitable, and reject the rest.")

What is the logical basis for his justification in telling only good stories to the young? What is the role of religion in the ideal education of rulers? [Insofar as "impiety" may well be an accusation against Socrates, you may wish to pay special attention to his views on the gods and religion.] How does Socrates justify the ruler's telling of lies to those being ruled? How does he justify censorship? Of literature? Of music?

Distribution of Roles

After the discussion, the roles for the Athens game will be randomly distributed to all students. You should read your role privately several times and put it away. You should not share it with anyone else.

After the roles have been distributed and read, the Gamemaster will conduct the LOTTERY FOR POSITIONS. Every student will put her name on a piece of paper. The list of possible openings is as follows:

Position	Number Selected, assuming six public sessions	Tenure
Assembly President of the Day	SIX	One class, set at outset of game
Herald	SIX	One class, set at outset
Archon	Three or Four	Duration of game, as needed
Replacements (AP, archons, Heralds)	One of Each	Duration of game, as needed

The "replacements" will function if the Assembly President for the Day or the Herald for the Day, fails to be present in class. The Gamemaster will randomly assign Athenian citizens (not the metic leader) to these positions.

After the positions have been distributed, some member of each of the four major factions (Radical Democrats, Moderate Democrats, Oligarchs, and Socratics) should identify himself (we need a volunteer!) and propose to convene a gathering either in one corner of the room, or perhaps in the café below, or at a comfortable place outside. You might wish to let the Gamemaster, who may have some advice, know where you're going. At these factional meetings, each party must choose a leader, though it may be only temporary. The Democratic Party of Athens should by all rights democratically **elect** their leader (Thrasybulus); the student chosen to be Thrasybulus should approach the Gamemaster for a special role sheet. The Oligarchs, by all rights, might choose the student who is of the most noble family background, steeped in tradition (or perhaps in wealth). The members of the Socratic Party should choose that person who, as evidenced by her devoted and rigorous pursuit of truth, would best exemplify the qualities of a philosopher (and, thus, a leader). (Good luck, here!) At this first factional get-together, you should form the social bond that will allow you to cohere quickly and withstand the likely strain that will come in the weeks ahead. Exchange phone numbers and e-mail addresses. Perhaps choose a place to gather after class. Have a cup of coffee.

The Indeterminates are different. They are not a party or collective entity. Their objectives may be utterly dissimilar. Thus while the other two groups are happily bonding, the Indeterminates will likely mill about confusedly.

Warning to Indeterminates: Because you do not yet know enough about what's going on, be cautious. Repeat: you do not understand the game or the concept of this particular game yet. This will take some time. But until you know what you're doing, don't say too much to anyone about your role. You may not even wish to identify yourself in relation to your public persona, although this will get out sooner or later. If anyone asks who you are and what you stand for, you have a right to be wary. You may find it more difficult to attain your objectives if others can look "into your soul," as it were. The Gamemaster expects you to be a bit nervous and confused. While the others will take comfort in having a fixed set of beliefs, you will doubtless be unsettled by your indeterminate role. As Socrates maintained, it is more difficult to question than to believe. Yet take heart. What you decide will determine the outcome of the entire game; everyone will hang on your words and solicit your opinions (and votes). But for a time you are to listen and read and think. And you should speak or email the Gamemaster.

Ten minutes before the end of class, everyone should return to the classroom, though you should now sit with your faction. The Radical Democrats may wish to sit adjacent to the Moderate Democrats, and the Oligarchs to the Socratics. The factions will introduce their chosen leaders.

CLASS 3: GAME INTRODUCTION

Brief discussion of Plato's Republic (Books IV-V) and Documents

Plato, *The Republic*: Parts IV and V
Also: read the entire **Documents Section** of the Game Packet.

Class Discussion Questions

Why must the guardians be celibate? What, in the absence of fleshly satisfactions and even possession of private property, are the guardians to be doing?

What is the myth of the metals and what are its implications?

Socrates says that a just state must have the qualities of "wisdom, courage, self-discipline, and justice." How does his ideal state exemplify these traits? What does he mean by the "unity of parts"? Ponder, in relation to the last question, the "man standing still but flapping his arms": what is the point of this?

Factional meetings

For thirty or so minutes, the four factions will meet separately, at a location of their own choosing (let the Gamemaster know where). For the Indeterminates: the Gamemaster will immediately meet with each Indeterminate separately.

SUMMARY TABLE: DATE AND SEQUENCE OF CLASSES

DATE	Session No.	Activities: Gamemaster	Activities: Assembly OR *Dikasterion*	Assembly Pres. / Herald of Day (X)	Written assignments
	1	Introduction to Course			
	2	Discussion: *Republic;* Distribution of Roles; Lottery for offices			
	3	Discussion: Republic	Factional meetings		
	4		PUBLIC SESSION 1	Assembly Pres #1 presides*	1st papers: at least one from all factions
	5		PUBLIC SESSION 2	AP # 2 presides	1st papers: one from all factions; 2 indeterminates
	6		FULL SESSION 3	AP #3 presides	Final first paper submissions (remainder of students)
	7		FULL SESSION 4	AP #4 presides/ Ostracism vote (end)	2nd papers: at least one from all factions
	8		FULL SESSION 5	AP #5 presides	Second papers: one from all factions; 2 indeterminates
	9		FULL SESSION 6	AP #6 presides	Second papers: remainder of all students
	END	INTRO: GAME 2			

*Note: In the event of a trial, as approved by Gamemaster, an archon will be assigned some of the class time otherwise scheduled for the Assembly meeting.

Elasticity of Time, and Who Knows What and When?

The Assembly of Athens met about every ten days. However, the passage of time during the game is more elastic. Students can fairly assume that **at least** ten days in real time pass between class sessions. But it is possible that considerably more time may elapse; the Gamemaster may provide some guidance on such matters. (For example, the Assembly may vote to begin immediate construction of a fleet of *triremes*. Whether these ships will be ready to sail by the **next** session is a matter to be determined by the Gamemaster.)

But remember: although Reacting time is elastic, it is not reversible. That is, the game is set in the fall of 403 B.C. and afterwards. No one can refer to things that have not yet occurred. If, for example, you allude to the American Congress, your auditors will think you mad. Perhaps they will ostracize you as someone whose rantings offend the gods. What knowledge, then, is common to the entire group?

Things You Should Know

GREEK MYTHOLOGY

Zeus, Demeter, Herakles (Hercules). Any compendium of Greek "mythology" will prove useful. For on-line, and brief, accounts of the latter, try: www.perseus.tufts.edu, and follow the index to stories about Herakles.

ANCIENT TEXTS: HOMER AND HESIOD

Related to the above are the ancient texts of Homer, especially the *Iliad* and *Odyssey*. Greek and English on-line versions of the *Iliad* and *Odyssey* are available at the Perseus website. For information on daily life, you may wish to consult Hesiod's *Works and Days*. You can find these texts—in English and Greek—on line at the www.perseus.tufts.edu website.

CONTEMPORARY TEXTS (WRITTEN BETWEEN 430 B.C. AND 403 B.C.)

Insofar as you were probably born around 433 B.C., and because during the following decades Athens shifted from a predominantly oral tradition to a written tradition, writing has become all the rage during your lifetime. The more important books and copies of important speeches are copied out and sold in the Agora. The texts available to you are of several types:

Plays

The chief tragic poet of your era is Euripides, who died just three years ago; his *Trojan Women* (415 B.C.) indirectly addresses issues surrounding the Athenian campaign to conquer Sicily of that year. Your lifetime has also witnessed the perfection of comedy in the work of Aristophanes, now in his forties. His protagonist is characteristically consumed with some goof-ball notion, which spoofs real characters and situations. His *Clouds* (423 B.C.) satirizes Socrates and the sophists; *Wasps* (422), the law courts and legal profession; *The Knights* (424), the appeal of demagogues to the Assembly; *Lysistrata* (411 B.C.), women's decision to boycott sexual relations with their husbands to bring an end to war; *Frogs*, the hidebound conservativism of the people, and so on. [His major plays are also available in full-text versions at the Perseus Project website.]

Speeches to the Assembly and Law Courts

More than a few scholarly souls copied out the better speeches delivered in the Assembly and law courts. One of the most diligent was Thucydides, who has begun assembling the speeches pertaining to the Peloponnesian war into a book, which covers the years from 431 B.C., when the war began, to 411 B.C. You have access to an early draft of the book, *The History of the Peloponnesian War*. [See, again, the Perseus Project website, as above.] His rendering of major speeches, such as Pericles' Funeral Oration and the account of the destruction of the Athenian expedition to Sicily, also appear in the appendix section of this booklet.

Some important law speeches are also included in the packet. One of the most famous legal orators, Lysias, has published many of his speeches [which were recovered in papyrii, and are available on the Perseus Project website].

The Words of Socrates

Socrates, perhaps the cleverest (or the most foolish) man in all Greece, talks incessantly to nearly anyone who will listen in the Agora. He does not write. But his younger disciples are among those who have caught the writing disease, and several diligently copy down his more interesting dialogues.

Somehow, you have gained access to their notes, which doubtless will be published. Plato's *Republic* is [for the purpose of the game] a faithful account of Socrates's words, and his vision of a utopia. It is a long and difficult work; many readers, after slogging through a few pages, find its dialogic structure simplistic and the analogies unsatisfying. They may imagine that they can be effective leaders in the Assembly and law courts without paying it much heed. They are wrong. In the *Republic*, Plato/Socrates builds a formidable intellectual edifice.

The Oligarchical Worldview: Xenophon's Oeconomicus

Included as an appendix are selections from a Socratic dialogue, compiled /composed by Xenophon, between Socrates and an esteemed Oligarch. This dialogue outlines the gentlemanly precepts of the Oligarchical ethos. To understand the Oligarchical mindset, you must read this work.

ADVISORY ON THE TEXTS

You may be tempted to read only the texts that support your views. This is ill advised. You should read all of the texts. As the rhetorician Gorgias observed, it does not suffice to advance your **own** views. You must also anticipate the arguments of others and rebut them effectively.

THE WORLD CONTEXT: SPARTA, PERSIA

When you are seated in the Assembly or law courts, you may imagine that Athens is the whole world. This thought, however comforting, is untrue. Actions taken by the Assembly, and even by jurors in the law courts, have repercussions throughout Greece, and even beyond. For example, if the Assembly votes to send a naval expedition to the Ionian district, word of that action will spread quickly and stimulate debates throughout the Mediterranean and in Persia. Conversely, the death of a Persian king, a drought in Egypt, or a rebellion among the *helots* in Sparta—all of these distant (possible) events, and many others—could profoundly affect Athens.

The Gamemaster may choose to inform you of what's happening elsewhere; or he may not. The actions of the Athenian Assembly are publicly known; the decisions of a Spartan or Persian king may not be known to the people of Athens. Generally speaking, the Gamemaster would let all Athens know of what is going on elsewhere if it is likely that they would know it. The Gamemaster may convey some information to some players and not to others, if that, too, makes sense.

Individual Athenians [and students] cannot appropriate the voices of foreign statesmen. For example, students cannot assert as fact that the crops have failed in Egypt, or that the *helots* have incapacitated Sparta with a slave rebellion. Students may attempt to convey messages that might influence people beyond Athens. They can do so by sending letters (or e-mails) to the person involved via the Gamemaster, who will serve as intermediary. For example, if an Oligarch wants to persuade Aristophanes to write a play denouncing Thrasybulus, or if a Radical Democrat wants to write a letter to the Persian emperor in hope of winning him over to democracy, she may do so by drafting a letter (or an email) and sending it to such personages via Gamemaster. The Gamemaster may or may not bring back a response. Aristophanes may find the request preposterous, and a letter from Athens to the Persian court in Susa may not arrive. Students cannot presume or force any action by the Gamemaster.

Students are not allowed to send anonymous e-mails.

The Gamemaster controls what, if anything, is happening in the world beyond the Pnyx and the law courts. The Gamemaster will take such actions to enhance the historical verisimilitude of the game, to make it intellectually more stimulating, or to promote other objectives that students may find wholly unfathomable. This is a way of affirming that the past is complex and elusive; no one knows exactly what is happening and why.

The Gamemaster is obliged in at least one instance to mediate between Athens and the world beyond. If, for example, Athens sends a naval expedition to force the former Hellespontine tributary district to resume its payments, the Gamemaster will, after the final meeting of the Assembly, indicate whether the expedition succeeded. In this instance, and perhaps others, the Gamemaster may make use of dice. This, too, affirms that history is often contingent: chance does make a difference in human affairs.

Nevertheless, sometimes destiny needs human assistance. You may wish to persuade the Gamemaster to activate external forces. To that end, you need understand the world beyond Athens. The following paragraphs provide a mere outline of the most important forces. You may wish to conduct your own historical research, and submit it to the Gamemaster in support of your policy gambits. The Gamemaster, though omnipotent, is not omniscient.

Sparta: A Brief History

For the past century or so, the two great city-states of the Aegean were Athens and Sparta. In the 800s B.C., Sparta began its conquest of other peoples of the Peloponnesus, the peninsula at the southern tip of Greece. During the next century it conquered Messenia and forced its people into a form of serfdom. These serfs were known as *helots*, who were bound to the soil they worked This domination of the *helots* became a central fact of Spartan history, and a preoccupation of Spartan government and culture. Sparta's wealth derived from land and farming, its prowess at war from a well-disciplined army and the militarization of all aspects of society, and its political direction from a handful of powerful families (oligarchs). (A major region of Sparta was called Laconia. Thus the Spartans are sometimes identified as Lacedaemonians, after their territory.)

Around 700 B.C., a legendary (perhaps mythical) lawgiver, Lycurgus, proposed a constitution for Sparta. It provided for a dual kingship (giving each a right to command the army, so that one king could serve as a counterweight to the other); a council of aristocrats as guides, known as the Council of Elders, plus an Assembly, attended by all citizens. (Unlike the Athenian Assembly, the Spartan assembly did not make laws; nor did it allow every citizen to speak.)

After a bloody mass uprising of the *helots* in the mid-600s, Spartan society became more conservative. It became isolationist, and focused on agriculture rather than trade with other Greek communities. It also devised a militaristic ethic, imposing severe and protracted military training on all citizens, and a repressive system of control of the *helots*. By 500 B.C., Sparta had become the dominant military power in Greece.

When Persia invaded Greece, Athens and Sparta joined forces. In 480, the combined operations of the Athenian, Spartan, and other Greek navies destroyed the Persian fleet at Salamis, and the Persian army was shortly thereafter defeated and withdrawn. As Athens assumed leadership of the 150 city-states in the confederacy against Persia, Sparta grew more concerned. By the 450s, Sparta regarded Athenian imperialism as a threat to its own position. Because of its mighty fleet, Athens not only forced other states to make large tribute payments but it also often put into power the local democratic faction of these states. Sparta worried that this democratic ethos might somehow spread amongst its own *helots* and lead to a slave rebellion.

In 431 B.C. Athens and Sparta went to war. Known as the Peloponnesian War, it was the great event of classical Greek history.

Persia

Around 500 B.C., when Darius I was king, the Persian empire stretched from the Indus Valley westward to Libya. It was the largest empire the world had known. Persia expanded toward Europe and took control of the scores of Greek city-states that had been planted in Ionia (the western coast of what is now Turkey). In 499, when these city-states rebelled against Darius, Athens provided military assistance to the rebels. By 491, the Persians had dominated the Greeks of Ionia; Darius now resolved to punish Athens and conquer all Greece. The Athenians, abetted by Plataea, defeated Darius at Marathon in 490 B.C.. When Darius's son, Xerxes, attempted another conquest of Greece a decade later, it, too, was defeated. Over the course of the Peloponnesian War, Persia learned to work Greek cities against each other to its own advantage.

In recent years, a series of assassinations and coups have weakened Persia, whose leadership is now in a state of flux. But in 403 B.C., the Persian leader—perhaps Artaxerxes or perhaps his brother, Cyrus, who contend for the throne—doubtless is interested in reestablishing Persian influence in Ionia, the Aegean, the Black Sea, and northern Greece.

ATHENIAN HISTORY: A CHRONOLOGY

Pre 900 B.C.: Hereditary Aristocracy in Athens, and most Greek City States

During the period from about 700 to 500 B.C., many Greek city-states sent their surplus population to found colonies throughout the Mediterranean. Many fall into slavery or are exiled. Free farmers become increasingly fearful of their economic vulnerability, and of the unrestricted power of the aristocracies. Land shortage and craving for adventure leads to founding of Greek communities on lands washed by the Mediterranean. Many Greek states establish hundreds of Greek colonies nearly everywhere. Trade expands throughout Mediterranean.

During this period, most of the Greek settlements, really a patchwork of tribes, are ruled by **hereditary "big men."** Many of these communities become divided between oligarchical and democratic factions. In most Greek states, poor farmers become weaker, losing their land and rights.

600 B.C. Athens: *Tyranny of Pisistratus*

594:     In Athens, as class tensions lead to protracted civil war, an imaginative leader named Solon cancels debt and creates a Council of 400 to guide Athens: this is viewed as one of the earliest measures limiting the power of the oligarchs.

546:     **Pisistratus** (Pih-SIS-trah-tis) establishes self as tyrant in Athens, family as hereditary Tyranny.

Proto-Democracy: The Reforms of Kleisthenes (510-500 B.C.)

510:     Kleisthenes (KLIZE-the-neze), with Spartan aid, overthrows tyranny in Athens.

508:     Civil war, victory of demos.

507:     Kleisthenes's reforms: Weakening of aristocratic clans; greater political rights given to farmers, merchants, and artisans; governing council of aristocrats eliminated. Sparta's attempts to crush the proto-democracy fail.

500 (?): Pnyx built.

487:     Archons chosen by lot.

The Persian Threat Repulsed (490-480 B.C.)

500:     Persians attempt conquest of Naxos (island state in the Aegean).

499-6:   Ionian cities (of Greek settlement) revolt against Persian rule.

490:     Persian invasion of northern Greece, repulsed at Marathon (Athenian victory): 6,400 Persian dead, Athenian losses: 192.

490-80: Persians under Xerxes (ZERK-sees) prepare for huge invasion of Greece.

490-80: Themistocles (thih-MIHS-toe-kleze): persuades Athenians to build mighty Navy.

480:     Persians under Xerxes invade Greece; Persian navy enticed into Bay of Salamis (SAHL-eh-mss) and destroyed by combined Greek navies.

478:     Creation of Delian League (Confederacy); Greek city-states, under Athenian leadership, pool financial resources to oppose Persia.

Summary: The withdrawal of the Persian threat resulted in an intense rivalry for leadership within Greece between two city-states—Athens and Sparta. The conflict between Athens and Sparta was all the more acute because of their antithetical social and political systems.

Athenian riches were spent not only on defense—chiefly the construction of more *triremes* (and the vast sums necessary to pay the oarsmen) and the long, impregnable walls stretching from Piraeus to Athens—but also on temples, such as the magnificent Parthenon, and on theatres, majestic buildings such as the Acropolis, and also on works of art, including sculpture, plays, festivals and athletic games.

Democracy Institutionalized: Periclean Athens (451 B.C.- 431)

461:    Democratic revolution in Athens, under Pericles. Assembly sets policy.

457:    Archons (trial magistrates) chosen by lot.

450s: Payment of jurors instituted.

451:    Pericles' law of citizenship: expansion of democratic powers, full public debate of all issues; end of citizenship for metics.

440s: Most officials chosen by random lottery.

447:    Pericles proposes extensive building program.

438:    Parthenon completed.

430:    Rise of intellectual school of Sophism.

Summary: The rise of the democratic order in fifth-century Athens challenged the position of prominent citizens there and offended their notions of social and political order. Moreover, the success of Athenian democracy, and especially its newfound imperialism, alarmed the leaders of Sparta, which prided itself on not imposing tribute payments upon its weaker allies. Sparta and its allies formed the Peloponnesian League, which Sparta dominated, even so far as insisting that its allies be run by oligarchies. Athens, too, formed a military alliance. Inevitably, Sparta and Athens came to blows. This resulted in the great Peloponnesian war.

Back then—431 B.C.—Pericles had assured the Assembly that Athens would likely win a war against Sparta, because the Athenian treasury was filled with silver. Athens had the wherewithal to build a mighty fleet and powerful army and keep it in action for years; no other city-state possessed such wealth.

Peloponnesian War, First Phase: Athenian Advantage (431-421 B.C.)

431:    Outbreak of Peloponnesian War.

430:    Sparta invades Attica, where they will remain for years.

430-29: Plague decimates Athens.

429:     Death of Pericles, of plague; Plato born.

420s: Class wars in city-states throughout Greece (see J. Ober essay in this
         packet)

Summary of Phase 1: Once each year, usually after crops had been planted,
Spartan armies swarmed north from the Peloponnesus into Attica and drove the
farmers of Attica to seek refuge inside the great walls that protected Athens and
extended all the way to the port city of Piraeus. But while the Spartans ravaged
Attica, destroying crops and farms, they could not breach the walls of Athens.
While the Spartan army encamped beyond the Athenian walls, the Athenian fleet
dashed throughout the Aegean, staging raids on the Spartan coast or on cities that
had allied with Sparta. Because the enemies were evenly matched but mutually
invincible—the Athenians could not be defeated at sea, nor the Spartans on
land—this strange war lasted for years, with the Athenians getting slightly the
better of it.

Peloponnesian War, Second Phase: "Peace" of Nicias (421-415 B.C.)

421:     Peace of Nicias: Truce declared; Sparta and Athens not to fight each
         other. Intermittent and recurrent lapses.

Summary of Phase 2: In 421 both Athens and Sparta, exhausted, declared truce.
This was called the Peace of Nicias. Each city-state would cease fighting the
other, though Athens could expand its influence to the north, and Sparta, further
south. Meanwhile, many city states throughout Greece became embroiled in
local civil wars between democratic and oligarchic factions.

Peloponnesian War, Third Phase: The Sicilian Disaster (415-411B.C.)

415:     Athenian expedition to Sicily, later reinforced.

413:     Sparta invades Attica.

413:     Athenian navy and army destroyed in Sicily; tribute states stop payment
         to Athens.

412:     Spartan-Persian alliance: Persian money to build Spartan fleet; Spartan
         support for Persian advance in Ionia. Alliance is engineered by
         Alcibiades.

411:     Revolution in Athens. Sparta continues revolt in Euboea, a large island
         near Athens crucial to survival of city. Oligarchs establish the rule of the
         Four Hundred. Democratic counterrevolution, abetted by remnants of
         Athenian fleet in Samos and by Alcibiades, overthrows the Four
         Hundred (oligarchs). Democrats in Athens recall Alcibiades.

Summary of Phase 3: In 415, the Athenian assembly voted to send a huge
expedition of troops and sailors to Sicily to help an allied city-state (See Map A).
Sparta feared this expansion of Athenian naval power, and shortly after the

Athenian army and navy left for Sicily, Sparta sent an army into Attica: both sides had broken the truce.

End of Peloponnesian War: Sparta Victorious (410-404 B.C.)

407:    Lysander given command of Spartan fleet, and wins major victories in 406 and 405. **Athenian fleet annihilated at Aegispotami.** Loss of neighboring farmlands and Spartan blockade (preventing import of grain from Black Sea and Egypt).

404:    **Siege of Athens** (404). Widespread starvation; Athens surrenders to Sparta. The terms of surrender led to the dismantling of the long walls connecting Piraeus and Athens. (No longer could the Athenians and their army hide from the Spartans behind fortifications). The Spartans also seized most of what remained of the Athenian fleet. And, to the shock of most Athenians, the Spartans left a military garrison in Athens and installed a new government, run by oligarchs—powerful rich Athenians who opposed democratic rule. The Thirty execute some 1,500 democrats.

The Brief (Antidemocratic) Reign of the Thirty Tyrants (404 B.C.)

The Thirty Tyrants, led by the vitriolic antidemocrat, Critias (KRIHT-ee-us), first restricted the vote to those Athenian citizens who owned property (the Three Thousand, as they were called). Critias ruled that anyone **not** on the list possessed no legal rights whatsoever. But soon the Thirty Tyrants ceased referring to the Three Thousand and appropriated all political power to themselves. They claimed (and sometimes exercised) the power to execute summarily anyone who was not on the list of the Three Thousand. Few issues were even brought before the Assembly. The Thirty arrested and executed over a thousand Athenian citizens and exiled thousands more. Most of those who were executed had been prominent in democratic circles, but some were exiled or executed so that the Thirty could seize their lands.

Many democrats fled from the terror, but some regrouped and resolved to overthrow the Tyrants. They formed a small army and occupied a hilltop position on the Boetian border; the Thirty sent a much larger cavalry unit to dispossess the democrats, but were defeated, a shocking setback to the Thirty that resulted in further defections to the democrats. The democrats then craftily attacked Piraeus and drove the army of the Thirty from that city; the democrats now made preparations for an assault on the Tyrants in Athens. The democrats' prospects were promising until just a few weeks ago, when the Spartan garrison in Athens attacked the democrat exiles and inflicted heavy casualties on them. Then, King Pausanias of Sparta, decided to withdraw the Spartan garrison. The Thirty Tyrants fled. The democracy was restored.

MAP A: THE HELLENIC WORLD

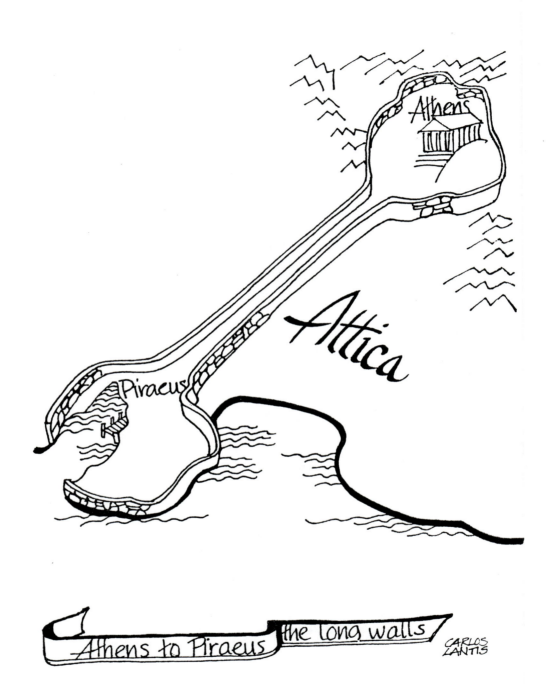

The Threshold of Democracy

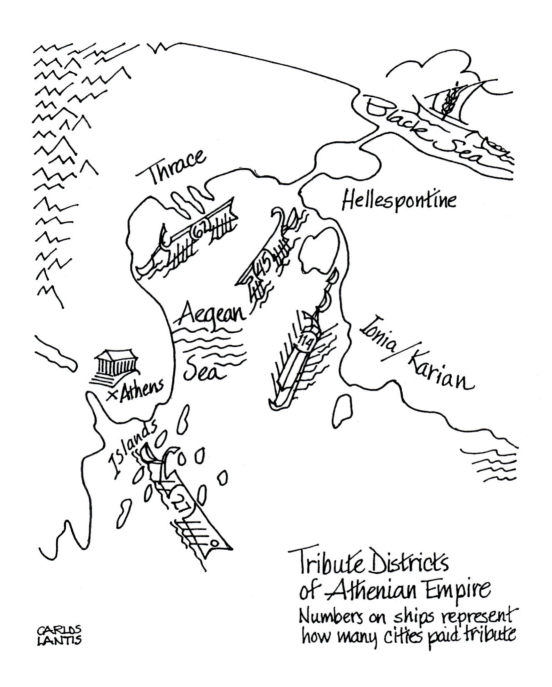

Tribute Districts
of Athenian Empire
Numbers on ships represent
how many cities paid tribute

CARLOS
LANTIS

APPENDIX A: Indeterminate Biographies (Public)

FISHMONGER

A hard-working and ambitious citizen, he works as a fishmonger in Piraeus. He is thirty-two. The young man's father was a stonemason; as a boy he worked with his father on repairing the long walls between Piraeus and Athens. When he was seventeen, he traveled from his home town of Pallene, near Marathon, to perform at the great city festival as one of the fifty members of his tribal chorus. During the weeks of training and competition in town he attracted the notice of two middle-aged men, who fell him love with him. Their quarrel, which ended in a fight, resulted in a lawsuit before the *dikasterion*. For a brief time, the young man was the subject of considerable enthusiastic discussion in the Agora. One of the older men ran a fish shop and hired the young man to work in it. When the young man married, he set up a fish stand in Piraeus, several blocks from the docks. He has a wife and three children. He owns no property and is among those classed as *thetes*. He has recently served as one of the 170 oarsmen on a *trireme*, the three-tiered warship that is the backbone of the navy. In recent years, he has earned more from his salary as a rower than from his work in the fish shop. His ship fought in several inconclusive engagements. His ship was in Piraeus for repairs when most of the Athenian fleet was destroyed at Aegispotami.

RETIRED SAILOR

Once a sailor, he is now forty-nine. His father was a farmer in rural Attica, who grew olive and fig trees. But the boy was the youngest of five brothers, and when he turned eighteen he went to work in Athens as an apprentice in pottery shop. He grew interested in painting the pottery, but found the work dull, and he volunteered for service in the Athenian navy.

Even before his training as a rower was complete, he was assigned to serve on a ship that was dispatched to help defend Corcyra, an island state in the Ionian Sea [433 B.C.]. Corcyra, which had entered into a protective alliance with Athens, was being blockaded by the navy of Corinth, a commercial rival of Athens. Corinth evidently was planning to conquer Corcyra. When the Athenian ships approached the coast of Corcyra, however, the Corinthian navy withdrew to the north.

When the Great Peloponnesian War began [431 B.C.], the boy was twenty-two. For a time, he had nothing to do. The Spartans and their allies, irrepressible on land, repeatedly crossed the Isthmus of Corinth into Attica, ravaging the farms and driving the entire population into Athens and Piraeus (connected by a great walled fortification). While the great plague decimated the people within Athens (430-429), the sailor was unaffected, for the mighty Athenian navy could go wherever it wished and plundered one after another town along the Peloponnesian coastline. During these expeditions, he was occasionally among the group that went ashore, burning homes and crops, and attacking Spartan outposts.

A truce with Sparta was signed in 421 but came undone three years later. By that time, though, his period of obligatory service had ended. Several brothers had died in the plague and the boy returned to the family farm.

In 415 Athens decided to extend its power deep into the Mediterranean by conquering Syracuse, a democracy, in Sicily: again, the "sailor" was exempted for reason of age. On the eve of the fleet's departure, someone mutilated the Hermae, the statuary incarnations of Hermes that protected all Athenian homes. (Hermes was the god of fertility; also, of course the god of commerce, cunning, and theft, a messenger among the gods who also conducted the dead to Hades.) The desecration was especially unsettling to the boy, and to many other Athenians as well, because Hermes—as messenger—was also the patron of travelers. The omens taken the next day were also unpromising. The sailor also feared the hubris of the enterprise—would the pride of the mighty Athenian fleet of 140 *triremes* offend the Gods? Now married and with children, he was relieved that he was not part of the expedition.

The expedition initially did not meet with success. Several days after the fleet had departed from Piraeus, Alcibiades, its leader, was recalled to answer charges that he was responsible for the desecration of the Hermae. He evaded his escorts and sought refuge in Sparta, to which he offered his services. Syracuse did not fall in 414, and Nicias, leader of the expedition, sent word to Athens that he desperately needed reinforcements.

The Assembly voted the requisite aid. This time no exemptions were allowed and the aging sailor—nearly forty—carried his oar to Piraeus and boarded his *trireme*, commanded by one of his wealthy farm neighbors. But when the fleet reached the waters off Sicily, it encountered a capable and determined Syracusan navy. In 413 the reinforced Athenian fleet was repeatedly attacked. In one engagement the sailor's ship was nearly rammed but at the last moment his *trierarch*—the commander of the *trireme*—executed a sudden turn; a Syracusan ship hit it a glancing blow, sheering off the oars on the other side. Water poured through the shattered hull, but the ship made it to the shore. The sailor survived. But by the end of the day, the Athenian fleet was destroyed, and the army was now marooned in Sicily.

The sailor joined up with the army of Nicias, huddled on the coast of Sicily. For months the army was harried, starved, and gradually destroyed. Hopelessly surrounded, it surrendered. Some men were butchered on the spot, including the *trierarch* of the sailor's ship. The sailor, like thousands of others, was kept for months in a huge quarry pit. Most died. Fortunately, however, the sailor, during his winter's shore leave, had watched nearly every play and had memorized some of the major speeches. It happened that the wealthy farmers of Sicily craved Athenian drama, and they longed to hear Euripides. They bought as slaves those captives who had been actors. The sailor persuaded one unlettered Sicilian that he was an actor—he rattled off some Euripides' speech and faked the rest) and was bought as a house slave. During an errand in the market of Syracuse, near the harbor, the sailor managed to stow away aboard a ship sailing to the Black Sea. Eventually, he made his way home to Athens. His story has been told frequently.

He can no longer work. He refuses to speak of his experiences in Sicily. For a more detailed account of the horrors endured by such as he, see Thucydides, "The Sicilian Expedition" [included in the documentary packet]. He now lives with his eldest daughter in Athens, who cares for him.

IMPOVERISHED FARMER

He is thirty-one. He has worked the land in Attica his father worked, trying to grow enough grapes to stay out of debt. In this, too, he resembles his father. His father wanted him to marry early so as to perpetuate the family cult, and he did so. His father chose the young man's bride, also a member of the tribe. The father became respected in tribal (or clan) matters and took prominent roles in the approved religious sects. The boy's military service in the Home Guard was uneventful; he spent much of his time repairing the fortifications along the Great Wall. When not obliged to man the walls, he attempted to farm the lands worked by his father, who died during the Great Plague. When the father died, the son dutifully made all the requisite offerings and prayers.

The impoverished farmer had three children, two of them sons. Two infant girls were exposed shortly after birth. This was necessary because he lacked money for their dowries.

But nearly every year the Spartans would come, their presence announced by the great cloud of smoke caused by the burning homes and crops. He would try to hide his livestock and valuables, but usually the Spartans, bred to hunger and thievery, would find everything and either eat it, steal it, or destroy it. Several years ago, he sold his slave to pay his debts.

Of his four sons, two died during the "starving time" of the siege last year. His wife, gravely ill, cannot work. A kinswoman, herself malnourished, helps with the farm.

He took out loans, but word is that he is a bad risk. If he cannot pay his loans, he fears the loss of his farm and, more importantly, loss of citizenship; he has heard of proposals to limit citizenship to those with productive land holdings!

MERCHANT SON

He is thirty years old, the son of a well-to-do grain importer. The father lives in a town house in Athens, with five servants, and also owns a family estate outside the walls of Athens in Agryle (Attica) and another in Thrace, which he acquired from the Athenian government after Thrace had been conquered. Both estates are worked by slaves. The son lives in Athens, under the loose and benevolent supervision of his father. At eighteen, he began his military training as *ephebe*, and took the requisite oath.

"I shall not dishonor the sacred arms I bear; I shall never desert my fellow-soldiers; I shall fight in the defence of my country and her sanctuaries; and I shall hand on to posterity, to the best of my strength and with all my comrades' help, a city in no way diminished but rather made greater and more powerful. I shall obey the magistrates, the laws now in force, and those that may duly be enacted henceforward; if any person attempts to subvert them, I shall use all my strength, and the assistance of all men, to prevent this. I shall honor the cult of my ancestors. To this oath I ask the following divinities to bear witness: Aglauros, Hestia, Enyo, Enyalios, Ares and Athena, Areia,

Zeus, Thallo, Auxo, Hegemone, Heracles, the Boundaries of my country, the spirits of Corn, Barley, Vines, Olives and Figs."

He completed his service within the usual two years. He purchased a splendid set of armor with gold studs appropriate for his station, but has neglected to keep it in good repair or polish it. When Athens was not at war, he traveled throughout Greece and the eastern Mediterranean, usually with his father's grain ships. When called to serve in the military, he fought as a *hoplite*, though he functioned less as an infantryman and more as a raider. Whenever the Spartans descended upon the farms of Attica, he and a small group would slip out of the fortifications and harass the Spartan marauders. Six years ago he and four others exhibited valor if little skill in a night raid against a small group of Phocians, allied to Sparta, who had encamped in Agryle, near what had once been his suburban home. His abdomen was pierced by a spear. The wound festered. For much of the next two years he was plagued with fevers and digestive ailments. He thus played no role during the great famine occasioned by the Spartan siege and subsequent surrender of Athens; nor was he active during the subsequent reign of terror of the Thirty Tyrants.

It is not known what he thought about the Thirty Tyrants; nor is it known what he thinks of the current democratic government.

Though his foreign travels were to help his father's business by meeting with suppliers and potential purchasers, the talk about Athens is that the young merchant has little interest in his father's business. He has learned many languages, which he can write as well as read, and he has an insatiable curiosity. He befriends prominent visitors to Athens. He has been seen chatting with various Sophists, and also with Socrates, though apparently he is a disciple of none. In fact, he chats with nearly anyone who is well-placed in politics and the military, in Athens and other city-states. He appears equally interested in all. Moreover, he has so far shown little inclination to pursue a career in politics. He has joined no party, has not sought to win prizes in athletics or preferment in any religious rituals or feasts, and has given no public speeches. He practices the prescribed rituals regularly and was initiated into the Eleusinian Mysteries, though he has taken no special functions in any of these. He seldom attends the *gymnasia*.

He is unmarried and seems to be closely attached to no person, male or female. His main social event, apart from meeting with prominent men on an individual basis, is the theatre, especially the old-style tragedies of Aeschylus, Sophocles, and Euripides. He spends much time reading and writing; little wonder his eyes are bad.

RICH ATHLETE

He is thirty, the son of a prominent aristocrat, who owns landed estates in Attica and several colonized provinces. The father owned six or seven hundred slaves. One estate is famous for raising prize-winning race-horses.

The boy was admired as an athlete. Though he did not compete in the pan-Hellenic games, he took a second in the diaulos (quarter-mile run) at the games for the festival of Opora, the harvest goddess. This triumph was tainted, at least in the eyes of some, by his evident drunkenness during the ritual procession afterwards.

He proved an exemplary *ephebe*, and served in the cavalry afterwards, mounted upon one of his father's finest horses. He was an effective leader; during one raid he killed two Spartans single-handedly. In 409 another well-to-do young man charged him with murdering an insolent slave. The rich athlete spoke persuasively in his own defense and charged that his accuser was embittered at having lost a lover to him. The accuser failed to get the required 20% of jurors to vote for conviction, and thus was fined 1,000 drachma and deprived of the right of ever again making such an accusation.

In 404, after Sparta had destroyed the Athenian fleet and had laid siege to Athens by land, he gave an impassioned speech calling upon the people of Athens to resist Spartan tyranny. Nearly everyone was impressed, both by his words and handsome appearance. But by then, many in Athens were starving, and his words, coming from one as hardy and healthy as he, fell on deaf ears. Athens voted to surrender.

When Sparta installed the Thirty Tyrants, the rich athlete, fearing that his remarks against Sparta would be held against him, fled to a family estate toward the Hellespont, and across it as well.

He has returned just recently to Athens.

METIC

He is a metic, the son of a Thessian who worked as a steward for a prominent Athenian family. His father proved adept at numbers, managing the accounts of the farm and slaves in Attica and the real estate holdings in the city. He renegotiated the family's mortgages, and became active in financial circles in the Agora. He taught his son what he knew about numbers and business, and got him placed in the office of a grain merchant in Piraeus. The boy acquired capital of his own and started his own trading company, importing grain and exporting wine, olive oil, and manufactured goods. He has paid the obligatory taxes required of all metics, and he has also made special subscriptions to the war fund.

The metic was born in 443; this was, unfortunately, eight years after the citizenship laws [451 B.C.] which restricted Athenian citizenship to those whose parents were both citizens. Critias and the Thirty Tyrants confiscated a number of estates of metics in Athens, but early in the civil war Thrasybulus and his democrats seized Piraeus. The metic sought out Thrasybulus and, it is rumored, loaned him 1,500 drachmas, which Thrasybulus used to buy armor and pay mercenaries.

The metic remains a powerful figure in financial circles.

BEARDED ARTISAN

He is sixty, a shoemaker, living in Athens. He attends to business carefully: during the war years, he learned how to make the leather straps and shields used in armor, and did a good business, especially with knights who sought his painstaking craftsmanship. They arranged for him to be exempt from military service.

He also did well during the interruptions in the Great War, for when Athens was at peace and the ships flocked into Piraeus, laden with goods, he supplied sandals and shoes for export. Yet, though business was good, he never greatly expanded operations, but remained in the same shop, year after year. (It is located near the tanneries.)

His prudence extended to marital matters. For many years he doubted that he had the money to marry; then, at long last, he married a poor woman half his age only five years ago. He has no children. He attends the games infrequently, but dutifully presents himself at various temples for the requisite services.

He has exhibited no interest in politics, or in one faction or another. His views are conventional. He is undistinguished and mostly goes unnoticed, apart from his beard, which flows nearly to his waist, prompting people to call him, "The Bearded Shoemaker."

MIDDLING FARMER

He is thirty-five, owner of a small farm in Attica, far southeast of Athens. Because his farm was somewhat remote, located in the rockier soil of the foothills, the Spartans did not raid it very often. He attributes his good luck to his scrupulous adherence to the demands of the Gods.

He did his military service as a *hoplite*, and in this was fortunate as well. Though he fought in several battles, he was never even wounded. He married a local woman, and they have five children, four of them boys.

But even the middling farmer's luck could not survive the debacle at Aegispotami two years ago, where some 180 ships of the Athenian fleet were destroyed. Then the Spartans poured across the Decelean Pass and, more determined than ever before, scourged the countryside. The middling farmer and his family left the farm and, like most other country people, crowded into Athens, living in hovels along the Great Wall. They managed to survive the starving time, though nearly all were emaciated, and they returned home after the Thirty Tyrants had been installed. The middling farmer's cousin was bailiff at an estate of one of the Thirty, and the bailiff spoke highly of the man. So the middling farmer was satisfied with the outcome, which promised some measure of stability in Athens.

But one of the Middling Farmer's clansmen had been a prominent democrat and someone—was it the cousin?--brought this to the attention of the Thirty, who summarily executed him and confiscated his property. Now that the democrats have returned to power, the bailiff has denounced the Thirty. He says that he spoke well of them only to save himself. The deme is in turmoil, with kinfolk suspecting each other of treachery—in the past, or pending. The issue divides cousins, brothers, and even spouses. The middling farmer's wife is the sister of the bailiff; the deme member who perished at the hands of the Thirty was his brother.

The crops this year look promising; the Middling Farmer continues to observe the requisite religious proprieties.

CARPENTER

This young man, just turned thirty, has worked at various trades, none of them with much distinction. During the past few years, he has tried his hand as a carpenter. He left Athens and traveled with a work group that undertook various projects, including stage construction for a theatre troop in Corinth. Last year, he returned to Athens and was hired to help rebuild the Pnyx, which the Thirty redesigned. (The new design shifted the position of the rostrum so that the Assembly would no longer look out upon the sea; the Thirty maintained that this view of the sea encouraged democratic imperialism.)

That construction project has been cancelled. Whether the carpenter has had military training, no one can recall.

He is not married.

Appendix B: Documents

FUNERAL ORATION OF PERICLES: DEFENSE OF DEMOCRACY

[Editor's Note: This oration was delivered by Pericles, the greatest leader of Athenian democracy in 431 B.C. He gave it to commemorate those Athenian soldiers who died in the first battle of the war against Sparta. The speech was recorded by Thucydides (471 B.C.—400 B.C.), author of the History of the Peloponnesian War. Thucydides's book, which covers the war from its outset in 431 until 411 B.C., is acknowledged as the first serious work of history. Thucydides was generally critical of Athenian democracy—he commenced compiling the volume in 404, after Athens had been defeated by Sparta. He maintained that democracy was only good as the leader who guided the Assembly. Pericles, he maintained, was a brilliant statesman, warrior, and democratic politician. After Pericles died, however, the collective judgment of the people failed repeatedly, or so Thucydides contends. But Thucydides is regarded as a founder of historical method because he seems to have been fair in reporting facts and speeches. This oration is perhaps the earliest extended defense of a democratic system.]

After the first deaths in the war with Sparta, Pericles, son of Xanthippus, was chosen to give the eulogy. When the proper time arrived, he advanced from the sepulchre to an elevated platform in order to be heard by as many of the crowd as possible, and spoke as follows:

'Most of my predecessors in this place have commended whoever makes this speech that it be part of the law, telling us that it is well that it should be delivered at the burial of those who fall in battle. For myself, I should have thought that the worth which had displayed itself in deeds, would be sufficiently rewarded by honors also shown by deeds; such as you now see in this funeral prepared at the people's cost. And I could have wished that the reputations of many brave men were not to be imperilled in the mouth of a single individual, to stand or fall according as he spoke well or ill. For it is hard to speak properly upon a subject where it is even difficult to convince your hearers that you are speaking the truth. On the one hand, the friend who is familiar with every fact of the story, may think that some point has not been set forth with that fulness which he wishes and knows it to deserve; on the other, he who is a stranger to the matter may be led by envy to suspect exaggeration if he hears anything above his own nature. For men can endure to hear others praised only so long as they can severally persuade themselves of their own ability to equal the actions recounted: when this point is passed, envy comes in and with it incredulity. However since our ancestors have stamped this custom with their approval, it becomes my duty to obey the law and to try to satisfy your several wishes and opinions as best I may.

'I shall begin with our ancestors: it is both just and proper that they should have the honour of the first mention on an occasion like the present. They dwelt in the country without break in the succession from generation to generation, and handed it down free to the present time by their valour. And if our more remote ancestors deserve praise, much more do our own fathers, who added to their inheritance the empire which we now possess, and spared no pains to be able to leave their acquisitions to us of the present generation. Lastly, there are few parts of our dominions that have not been augmented by those of us here, who are still more or less in the vigour of life; while the mother country has been furnished by us with everything that can enable her to depend on her own resources whether for war or for peace. That part of our history which tells of the military achievements which gave us our several possessions, or of the ready valor with which either we or our fathers stemmed the tide of Hellenic or foreign aggression, is a theme too familiar to my hearers for me to dilate on, and I shall therefore pass it by. But what was the road by which we reached our position, what the form of government under which our greatness grew, what the national habits out of which it sprang; these are questions which I may try to solve before I proceed to my panegyric upon these men; since I think this to be a subject upon which on the present occasion a speaker may properly dwell, and to which the whole assemblage, whether citizens or foreigners, may listen with advantage.

'Our constitution does not copy the laws of neighbouring states; we are rather a pattern to others than imitators ourselves. Its administration favours the many instead of the few; this is why it is called a democracy. If we look to the laws, the afford equal justice to all in their private differences; if to social standing, advancement in public life falls to reputation for capacity, class considerations not being allowed to interfere with merit; nor again does poverty bar the way, if a man is able to serve the state, he is not hindered by the obscurity of his condition. The freedom which we enjoy in our government extends also to our ordinary life. There, far from exercising a jealous surveillance over each other, we do not feel called upon to be angry with our neighbour for doing what he likes, or even to indulge in those injurious looks which cannot fail to be offensive, although they inflict no positive penalty. But all this ease in our private relations does not make us lawless as citizens. Against this fear is our chief safeguard, teaching us to obey the magistrates and the laws, particularly such as regard the protection of the injured, whether they are actually on the statute book, or belong to that code which, although unwritten, yet cannot be broken without acknowledged disgrace.

'Further, we provide plenty of means for the mind to refresh itself from business. We celebrate games and sacrifices all the year round, and the elegance of our private establishments forms a daily source of pleasure and helps to banish the spleen; while the magnitude of our city draws the produce of the world into our harbour, so that to the Athenian the fruits of other countries are as familiar a luxury as those of his own.

'If we turn to our military policy, there also we differ from our antagonists. We throw open our city to the world, and never by alien acts exclude foreigners from any opportunity of learning or observing, although the eyes of an enemy may occasionally profit by our liberality; trusting less in system and policy than to the native spirit of our citizens; while in education, where our rivals from their very cradles by a painful discipline seek after manliness, at Athens we live exactly as we please, and yet are just as ready to encounter every legitimate danger. In proof of this it may be noticed that the Lacedaemonians do not invade our country alone, but bring with them all their confederates; while we Athenians advance unsupported into the territory of a neighbour, and fighting upon a foreign soil usually vanquish with ease men who are defending their homes. Our united force was never yet encountered by any enemy, because we have at once to attend to our marine and to despatch our citizens by land upon a hundred different services; so that, wherever they engage with some such fraction of our strength, a success against a detachment is magnified into a victory over the nation, and a defeat into a reverse suffered at the hands of our entire people. And yet if with habits not of labour but of ease, and courage not of art but of nature, we are still willing to encounter danger, we have the double advantage of escaping the experience of hardships in anticipation and of facing them in the hour of need as fearlessly as those who are never free from them.

'Nor are these the only points in which our city is worthy of admiration. We cultivate refinement without extravagance and knowledge without effeminacy; wealth we employ more for use than for show, and place the real disgrace of poverty not in owning to the fact but in declining the struggle against it. Our public men have, besides politics, their private affairs to attend to, and our ordinary citizens, though occupied with the pursuits of industry, are still fair judges of public matters; for, unlike any other nation, regarding him who takes no part in these duties not as unambitious but as useless, we Athenians are able to judge at all events if we cannot originate, and instead of looking on discussion as a stumbling-block in the way of action, we think it an indispensable preliminary to any wise action at all. Again, in our enterprises we present the singular spectacle of daring and deliberation, each carried to its highest point, and both united in the same persons; although usually decision is the fruit of ignorance, hesitation of reflexion. But the palm of courage will surely be adjudged most justly to those, who best know the difference between hardship and pleasure and yet are never tempted to shrink from danger. In generosity we are equally singular, acquiring our friends by conferring not by receiving favours. Yet, of course, the doer of the favour is the firmer friend of the two, in order by continued kindness to keep the recipient in his debt; while the debtor feels less keenly from the very consciousness that the return he makes will be a payment, not a free gift. And it is only the Athenians who, fearless of consequences, confer their benefits not from calculations of expediency, but in the confidence of liberality.

'In short, I say that as a city we are the school of Hellas; while I doubt if the world can produce a man, who where he has only himself to depend upon, is equal to so many emergencies, and graced by so happy a versatility as the Athenian. And that is no mere boast thrown out for the occasion, but plain matter of fact, the power of the state acquired by these habits proves. For Athens alone of her contemporaries is found when tested to be greater than her reputation, and alone gives no occasion to her assailants to blush at the antagonist by whom they have been worsted, or to her subjects to question her title by merit to rule. Rather, the admiration of the present and succeeding ages will be ours, since we have not left our power without witness, but have shown it by mighty proofs; and far from needing a Homer for our panegyrist, or other of his craft whose verses might charm for the moment only for the impression which they gave to melt at the touch of fact, we have forced every sea and land to be the highway of our daring, and everywhere, whether for evil or for good, have left imperishable monuments behind us. Such is the Athens for which these men, in the assertion of their resolve not to lose her, nobly fought and died; and well may every one of their survivors be ready to suffer in her cause.

'Indeed if I have dwelt at some length upon the character of our country, it has been to show that our stake in the struggle is not the same as theirs who have no such blessings to lose, and also that the panegyric of the men over whom I am now speaking might be by definite proofs established. That panegyric is now in a great measure complete; for the Athens that I have celebrated is only what the heroism of these and their like have made her, men whose fame, unlike that of most Hellenes, will be found to be only commensurate with their deserts. And if a test of worth be wanted, it is to be found in their closing scene, and this not only in the cases in which it set the final seal upon their merit, but also in those in which it gave the first intimation of their having any. For there is justice in the claim that stedfastness in his country's battles should be as a cloak to cover a man's other imperfections; since the good action has blotted out the bad, and his merit as a citizen more than outweighed his demerits as an individual. But none of these allowed either wealth with its prospect of future enjoyment to unnerve his spirit, or poverty with its hope of a day of freedom and riches to temp him to shrink from danger. No, holding that vengeance upon their enemies was more to be desired than any personal blessings, and reckoning this to be the most glorious of hazards, they joyfully determined to accept the risk, to make sure of their vengeance and to let their wishes wait; and while committing to hope the uncertainty of final success, in the business before them they thought fit to act boldly and trust in themselves. Thus choosing to die resisting, rather than to live submitting, they fled only from dishonour, but met danger face to face, and after one brief moment, while at the summit of their fortune, escaped, not from their fear, but from their glory.

'So died these men as became Athenians. You, their survivors, must determine, to have as unfaltering a resolution in the field, though you may pray that it may have a happier issue. And not contented with ideas derived only from words of the advantages which are bound up with the defence of your country, though these would furnish a valuable text to a speaker even before an audience so alive to them as the present, you must yourselves realise the power of Athens, and feed your eyes upon her from day to day, till love of her fills your hearts' and then when all her greatness shall break upon you, you must reflect that it was by courage, sense of duty, and a keen feeling of honour in action that men were enabled to win all this, and that no personal failure in an enterprise could make them consent to deprive their country of their valour, but they laid it at her feet as the most glorious contribution they could offer. For this offering of their lives made in common by them all they each of them individually received that renown which never grows old, and for a sepulchre, not so much that in which their bones have been deposited, but that noblest of shrines wherein their glory is laid up to be eternally remembered upon every occasion on which deed or story shall call for its commemoration. For heroes have the whole earth for their tomb; and in lands far from their own, where the column with its epitaph declares it, there is enshrined in every breast a record unwritten with no tablet to preserve it, except that of the heart. These take as your model, and judging happiness to be the fruit of freedom and freedom of valour, never decline the dangers of war. For it is not the miserable that would most justly be unsparing of their lives; these have nothing to hope for: it is rather they to whom continued life may bring reverses as yet unknown, and to whom a fall, if it came, would be most tremendous in its consequences. And surely, to a man of spirit, the degradation of cowardice must be immeasurably more grievous than the unfelt death with strikes him in the midst of his strength and patriotism!

'Comfort, therefore, not condolence, is what I have to offer to the parents of the dead who may be here. Numberless are the chances to which, as they know, the life of man is subject; but fortunate indeed are they who draw for their lot a death so glorious as that which has caused your mourning, and to whom life has been so exactly measured as to terminate in the happiness in which it has been passed. Still I know that this is a hard saying, especially when those are in question of whom you will constantly be reminded by seeing in the homes of others blessings of which once you also boasted: for grief is felt not so much for the want of what we have never known, as for the loss of that to which we have been long accustomed. Yet you who are still of an age to beget children must bear up in the hope of having others in their stead; not only will they help you to forget those whom you have lost, but will be to the state at once a reinforcement and a security; for never can a fair or just policy be expected of the citizen who does not, like his fellows, bring to the decision the interests and apprehensions of a father. While those of you who have passed your prime must congratulate yourselves with the thought that the best part of your life was fortunate, and that the brief span that remains will be cheered by the fame of the departed. For it is only the love of honour that never grows old; and honour it is, not gain, as some would have it, that rejoices the heart of age and helplessness.

'Turning to the sons or brothers of the dead, I see an arduous struggle before you. When a man is gone, all are wont to praise him, and should your merit be ever so transcendent, you will still find it difficult not merely to overtake, but even to approach their renown. The living have envy to contend with, while those who are no longer in our path are honoured with a goodwill into which rivalry does not enter. On the other hand, if I must say anything on the subject of female excellence to those of you who will now be in widowhood, it will be all comprised in this brief exhortation. Great will be your glory in not falling short of your natural character; and greatest will be hers who is least talked of among the men whether for good or for bad.

'My task is now finished. I have performed it to the best of my ability, and in word, at least, the requirements of the law are now satisfied. If deeds be in question, those who are here interred have received part of their honours already, and for the rest, their children will be brought up till manhood at the public expense; the state thus offers a valuable prize, as the garland of victory in this race of valour, for the reward both of those who have fallen and their survivors. And where the rewards for merit are greatest, there are found the best citizens.

'And now that you have brought to a close your lamentations for your relatives, you may depart.'

ATHENAGORAS: ON THE MERITS OF DEMOCRACY AND THE CONSPIRACY AGAINST IT (415 B.C.)

[Editor's Note: In the fateful Assembly meeting of 415 B.C., Athenagoras speaks in favor of the expedition to Sicily. His argument is that democracy is capable of prosecuting war, even distant wars. He rebuts the wealthy citizens who speak against it, and alludes to a conspiracy to undermine Athenian democracy by criticizing the competence of the Assembly and those who lead it. This speech, too, comes from Thucydides's History (Book VI).]

Meanwhile Athenagoras, the leader of the people and very powerful at that time with the masses, came forward and spoke as follows:

'For the Athenians: some say that they are misguided by those who speak at Assembly meetings such as this one: but those who make such accusations are either cowards or traitors to Athens. As for those who carry such dire warnings and fill you with so much alarm, I wonder less at their audacity than at their folly, for we see through them. The fact is that they have their private reasons to be afraid, and wish to throw the city into consternation. Their alarming reports about Sicily do not arise of themselves, but are concocted by men who are always causing agitation. However, if you are well advised, you will not be guided in your calculation of probabilities by what these persons tell you, but by what shrewd men and of large experiences, as I esteem the Athenians to be, would be likely to do. . . . Nor is this the first time that I see these persons, when they cannot resort to deeds, trying by such stories and by others even more abominable to frighten your people and get into their hands the government: it is what I see always. And I cannot help fearing that trying so often they may one day succeed, and that we, as long as we do not feel the smart, may prove too weak for the task of preventing such persons from seizing power.

'The result is that our city is rarely at rest, but is subject to constant troubles and to contests as frequent against herself as against the enemy, not to speak of occasional tyrannies and infamous conspiracies against the democracy. However, I will try if you will support me, to let nothing of this happen in our time, by gaining you, the many, and by chastising the authors of such machinations, not merely when they are caught in the act—a difficult feat to accomplish—but also for what they have the wish though not the power to do; as it is necessary to punish an enemy not only for what he does, but also beforehand for what he intends to do. . .

'It will be said, perhaps, that democracy is neither wise nor equitable, but that the holders of property are also the best fitted to rule. I say, on the contrary, first, that the word *demos*, or people, includes the whole state, oligarchy only a part; next, that if the best guardians of property are the rich, and the best counsellors the wise, none can hear and decide so well as the many; and that all these talents, severally and collectively, have their just place in a democracy. But an oligarchy gives the many their share of the danger, and not content with the largest part takes and keeps the whole of the profit; and this is what the powerful and young among you aspire to, but in a great city cannot possibly obtain.

'But even now, foolish men, most senseless of all the Hellenes that I know, if you have no sense of the wickedness of your designs, or most criminal if you have that sense and still dare to pursue them, - even now, if it is not a case for repentance, you may still learn wisdom, and thus advance the interest of the country, the common interest of us all. Reflect that in the country's prosperity the men of merit in your ranks will have a share and a larger share than the great mass of your fellow-country-men, but that if you have other designs you run a risk of being deprived of all; and desist from reports like these, as the people know your object and will not put up with it. If the Athenians arrive, this city will repulse them in a manner worthy of itself; we have, moreover, generals who will see to this matter. And if nothing of this be true, as I incline to believe, the city will not be thrown into a panic by your intelligence, or impose upon itself a self-chosen servitude by choosing you for its rulers; the city itself will look into the matter, and will judge your words as if they were acts, and instead of allowing itself to be deprived of its liberty by listening to you, will strive to preserve that liberty, by taking care to have always at hand the means of making itself respected.'

Such were the words of Athenagoras.

ALCIBIADES AT SPARTA, ALSO THUCYDIDES, BOOK VI (ANTI-DEMOCRACY)

[Editor's Note: Alcibiades, having departed for Sicily with Nicias, received word that he was being recalled to Athens to stand trial for his alleged destruction of the Hermes, the religious icons placed outside most Athenian homes. Alcibiades escaped from the officers who were to bring him back for trial, and he heads straight to Sparta. In this speech, Alcibiades repudiates the democracy of Athens and proclaims his newfound allegiance to Sparta. He also advises the Spartans to send military advisers to Sicily to assist in the defeat of the oncoming Athenian expedition; he further urges the Spartans to strike at Attica, establishing a Spartan garrison on the Decelean pass that commands entry into Attica. Here he denounces Athenian democracy.]

'Those [Spartans here] who judged me unfavorably, because I leaned rather to the side of the commons [in Athens], must not think that their dislike is any better founded. We have always been hostile to tyrants, and all who oppose arbitrary power are called commons; hence we continued to act as leaders of the multitude; besides which, as democracy was the government of the city, it was necessary in most things to conform to established conditions. However, we endeavored to be more moderate than the licentious temper of the times; and while there were others, formerly as now, who tried to lead the multitude astray, the same who banished me, our party was that of the whole people, our creed being to do our part in preserving the form of government under which the city enjoyed the utmost greatness and freedom, and which we had found existing. As for democracy, the men of sense among us knew what it was, and I perhaps as well as any, as I have the more cause to complain of it; but there is nothing new to be said of an acknowledged folly--meanwhile we did not think it safe to alter it under the pressure of your hostility.

You have thus heard the history of the present expedition from the man who most exactly knows what our objects were; and the remaining generals will, if they can, carry these out just the same. But that the states in Sicily must succumb if you do not help them, I will now show. Meanwhile you must carry on the war here more openly, that the Syracusans seeing that you do not forget them, may put heart into their resistance, and that the Athenians may be less able to reinforce their armament. You must fortify Decelea in Attica, the blow of which the Athenians are always most afraid and the only one that they think they have not experienced in the present war; the surest method of harming an enemy being to find out what he most fears, and to choose this means of attacking him, since every one naturally knows best his own weak points and fears accordingly. The fortification in question, while it benefits you, will create difficulties for your adversaries, of which I shall pass over many, and shall only mention the chief. Whatever property there is in the country will most of it become yours, either by capture or surrender; and the Athenians will at once be deprived of their revenues from the silver mines at Laurium, of their present gains from their land and from the law courts, and above all of the revenue from their allies, which will be paid less regularly, as they lose their awe of Athens, and see you addressing yourselves with vigor to the war. The zeal and speed with which all this shall be done depends, Lacedaemonians, upon yourselves; as to its possibility, I am quite confident, and I have little fear of being mistaken.

Meanwhile I hope that none of you will think any the worse of me if after having hitherto passed as a lover of my country, I now actively join its worst enemies in attacking it, or will suspect what I say as the fruit of an outlaw's enthusiasm. I am an outlaw from the iniquity of those who drove me forth, not, if you will be guided by me, from your service: my worst enemies are not you who only harmed your foes, but they who forced their friends to become enemies; and love of country is what I do not feel when I am wronged, but what I felt when secure in my rights as a citizen. Indeed I do not consider that I am now attacking a country that is still mine; I am rather trying to recover one that is mine no longer; and the true lover of his country is not he who consents to lose it unjustly rather than attack it, but he who longs for it so much that he will go all lengths to recover it. For myself, therefore, Lacedaemonians, I beg you to use me without scruple for danger and trouble of every kind, and to remember the argument in every one's mouth, that if I did you great harm as an enemy, I could likewise do you good service as a friend, inasmuch as I know the plans of the Athenians, while I only guessed yours. For yourselves I entreat you to believe that your most capital interests are now under deliberation; and I urge you to send without hesitation the expeditions to Sicily and Attica; by the presence of a small part of your forces you will save important cities in that island, and you will destroy the power of Athens both present and prospective; after this you will dwell in security and enjoy the supremacy over all Hellas, resting not on force but upon consent and affection.'

XENOPHON, HELLENICA: CRITIAS, ON THE FAILINGS OF DEMOCRACY

[Editor's Note: Xenophon, a historian and soldier, wrote a history of Hellenica—of Greece—after 411 B.C. (This was the year that Thucydides's history ended. The paragraphs that follow are set in 404, after Athens has surrendered and the Spartan army has installed the Thirty Tyrants. Critias, leader of the Thirty, has outlined his plan for harsh measures against the democratic leaders, and also his intention of restricting political rights to those who own property. Indeed, he makes it clear that he wants his thirty allies alone to rule Athens. On these matters, he is opposed by Theramenes, a Moderate. Xenophon begins:]

Now in the beginning Critias and Theramenes were agreed in their policy and friendly; but when Critias showed himself eager to put many to death, because, for one thing, he had been banished by the democracy, Theramenes opposed him, saying that it was not reasonable to put a man to death because he as honored by the commons, provided he was doing no harm to the aristocrats. "For," said he, "you and I also have said and done many things for the sake of winning the favor of the city."

Critias responds by saying that the enemies of oligarchy must be eliminated.

"Gentlemen of the Senate [a new governmental body composed of an elite], if anyone among you thinks that more people than is fitting are being put to death, let him reflect that where governments are changed these things always take place; and it is inevitable that those who are changing the government here to an oligarchy should have most numerous enemies, both because the state is the most populous of the Greek states and because the property-less Athenians have been bred up in a condition of freedom for the longest time. Now we, believing that for men like ourselves, democracy is a grievous form of government. If we find anyone opposed to the oligarchy, so far as we have the power we put him out of the way; but in particular we consider it to be right that, if any one of our own number is harming this order of things, he should be punished.

"Now in fact we find this man Theramenes trying, by what means he can, to destroy both ourselves and you. As proof that this is true you will discover, if you consider the matter, that no one finds more fault with the present proceedings than Theramenes here, or offers more opposition when we wish to put some demagogue out of the way. Now if he had held these views from the beginning, he was, to be sure, an enemy, but nevertheless he would not justly be deemed a scoundrel. In fact, however, he was the very man who took the initiative in the policy of establishing a cordial understanding with the Lacedaemonians; he was the very man who began the overthrow of the democracy, and who urged you most to inflict punishment upon those who were first brought before you for trial; but now, when you and we have manifestly become hateful to the democrats, he no longer approves of what is going on,--just so that he may get on the safe side again, and that we may be punished for what has been done. Therefore he ought to be punished, not merely as an enemy, but also as a traitor both to you and to ourselves. And treason is a far more dreadful thing than war, inasmuch as it is harder to take precaution against the hidden than against the open danger, and a far more hateful thing, inasmuch as men make peace with enemies and become their trustful friends again, but if they catch a man playing the traitor, they never in any case make peace with that man or trust him thereafter. It is true, of course, that all sorts of changes in government are attended by loss of life, but you, thanks to your changing sides so easily, share the responsibility, not merely for the slaughter of a large number of oligarchs by the commons, but also for the slaughter of a large number of democrats by the aristocracy. . .

"Now when a man clearly shows that he is always looking out for his own advantage and taking no thought for honour or his friends, how in the world can it be right to spare him? ought we not surely, knowing of his previous changes, to take care that he shall not be able to do the same thing to us also? We therefore arraign him on the charge of plotting against and betraying both ourselves and you. And in proof that what we are thus doing is proper, consider this fact also. The constitution of the Lacedaemonians is, we know, deemed the best of all constitutions. Now in Lacedaemon if one of the ephors should undertake to find fault with the government and to oppose what was being done instead of yielding to the majority, do you not suppose that he would be regarded, not only by the ephors themselves but also by all the rest of the state, as having merited the severest punishment? Even so you, if you are wise, will not spare this Theramenes, but rather yourselves; for to leave him alive would cause many of those who hold opposite views to yours to cherish high thoughts, while to destroy him would cut off the hopes of them all, both within and without the city.

[Theramenes replies:]

I do not wonder, however, that Critias has misunderstood the matter; for when these events took place, it chanced that he was not here; he was establishing a democracy in Thessaly along with Prometheus, and arming the serfs against their masters. God forbid that any of the things which he was doing there should come to pass here. I quite agree with him, however, on this point, that if anyone is desirous of deposing you from your office and is making strong those who are plotting against you, it is just for him to incur the severest punishment. But I think you can best judge who it is that is doing this, if you will consider the course which each of us two has taken and is now taking.] Well then, up to the time when you became members of the Senate and magistrates were appointed and the notorious informers were brought to trial, all of us held the same views; but when these Thirty began to arrest men of worth and standing, then I, on my side, began to hold views opposed to theirs. For when Leon the Salaminian was put to death,--a man of capacity, both actually and by repute,--although he was not guilty of a single act of wrong-doing, I knew that those who were like him would be fearful, and, being fearful, would be enemies of this government. I also knew, when Niceratus, the son of Nicias, was arrested,--a man of wealth who, like his father, had never done anything to curry popular favour,--that those who were like him would become hostile to us.   And further, when Antiphon, who during the war supplied from his own means two fast-sailing *triremes*, was put to death by us, I knew that all those who had been zealous in the state's cause would look upon us with suspicion. I objected, also, when they said that each of us must seize one of the resident aliens; for it was entirely clear that if these men were put to death, the whole body of such aliens would become enemies of the government. [2.3.41] I objected likewise when they took away from the people their arms, because I thought that we ought not to make the state weak; for I saw that, in preserving us, the purpose of the Lacedaemonians had not been that we might become few in number and unable to do them any service; for if this had been what they desired, it was within their power, by keeping up the pressure of famine a little while longer, to leave not a single man alive.

"He dubs me `Buskin,' because, as he says, I try to fit both parties. But for the man who pleases neither party,--what in the name of the gods should we call him? For you in the days of the democracy were regarded as the bitterest of all haters of the commons, and under the aristocracy you have shown yourself the bitterest of all haters of the better classes. But I, Critias, am forever at war with the men who do not think there could be a good democracy until the slaves and those who would sell the state for lack of a shilling should share in the government, and on the other hand I am forever an enemy to those who do not think that a good oligarchy could be established until they should bring the state to the point of being ruled absolutely by a few. But to direct the government in company with those who have the means to be of service, whether with horses or with shields,1--this plan I regarded as best in former days and I do not change my opinion now. [2.3.49] And if you can mention any instance, Critias, where I joined hands with demagogues or despots and undertook to deprive men of standing of their citizenship, then speak. For if I am found guilty either of doing this thing now or of ever having done it in the past, I admit that I should justly suffer the very uttermost of all penalties and be put to death."

"When with these words he ceased speaking and the Senate had shown its good will by applause, Critias, realizing that if he should allow the Senate to pass judgment on the case, Theramenes would escape, and thinking that this would be unendurable, went and held a brief consultation with the Thirty, and then went out and ordered the men with the daggers to take their stand at the railing1 in plain sight of the Senate.

"Then he came in again and said: "Senators, I deem it the duty of a leader who is what he ought to be, in case he sees that his friends are being deceived, not to permit it. I, therefore, shall follow that course. Besides, these men who have taken their stand here say that if we propose to let a man go who is manifestly injuring the oligarchy, they will not suffer us to do so. Now it is provided in the new laws that while no one of those who are on the roll of the Three Thousand may be put to death without your vote, the Thirty shall have power of life or death over those outside the roll. I, therefore," he said, "strike off this man Theramenes from the roll, with the approval of all the Thirty. That being done," he added, "we now condemn him to death."

LYSIAS 12, DEMANDING PUNISHMENT FOR ERATOSTHENES, OF THE THIRTY

[Editor's Note: Lysias reports on the trial of Eratosthenes, accused of collaborating with the Thirty, especially in squeezing protection money from metics and arresting others.]

For they sent many of the citizens into exile with the enemy; they unjustly put many of them to death, and then deprived them of burial; many who had full civic rights they excluded from the citizenship; and the daughters of many they debarred from intended marriage. And they have carried audacity to such a pitch that they come here ready to defend themselves, and state that they are guilty of no vile or shameful action. I myself could have wished that their statement were true; for my own share in that benefit would not have been of the smallest. But in fact they have nothing of the sort to show in regard either to the city or to me: my brother, as I said before, was put to death by Eratosthenes, who was neither suffering under any private wrong himself, nor found him offending against the State, but merely sought to gratify his own lawless passions. I propose to put him up on the dais and question him, gentlemen of the jury. For my feeling is this: even to discuss this man with another for his profit I consider to be an impiety, but even to address this man himself, when it is for his hurt, I regard as a holy and pious action. So mount the dais, please, and answer the questions I put to you.

Did you arrest Polemarchus or not?

Erastothenes: I was acting on the orders of the government, from fear.

Were you in the Council-chamber when the statements were being made about us?

E: I was.

Did you speak in support or in opposition of those who were urging the death sentence?

E: In opposition.

You were against taking our lives?

E: Against taking your lives.--In the belief that our fate was unjust, or just?--That it was unjust.

So then, most abandoned of mankind, you spoke in opposition to save us, but you helped in our arrest to put us to death! And when our salvation depended on the majority of your body, you assert that you spoke in opposition to those who sought our destruction; but when it rested with you alone to save Polemarchus or not, you arrested him and put him in prison. So then, because you failed to help him, as you say, by your speech in opposition, you claim to be accounted a good citizen, while for having apprehended him and put him to death you are not to give satisfaction to me and to this court!

And further, supposing he is truthful in asserting that he spoke in opposition, observe that there is no reason to credit his plea that he acted under orders. For I presume it was not where the resident aliens were concerned that they sought to put him to the proof.1 And then, who was less likely to be given such orders than the man who was found to have spoken in opposition and to have declared his opinion? For who was likely to be less active in this service than the man who spoke in opposition to the object that they had at heart? For had there been some stronger authority in the city, whose orders were given him to destroy people in defiance of justice, you might perhaps have some reason for pardoning him; but whom, in fact, will you ever punish, if the Thirty are to be allowed to state that they merely carried out the orders of the Thirty?

Eratosthenes, if you had been a good citizen, you ought far rather to have acted as an informant to those who were destined to an unjust death than to have laid hands on those who were to be unjustly destroyed. But the fact is that your deeds clearly reveal the man who, instead of feeling pain, took pleasure in what was being done; so that this court should take its verdict from your deeds, not from your words. . .We are told, indeed, that of the Thirty Eratosthenes has done the least harm, and it is claimed that on this ground he should escape; but is it not felt that for having committed more offences against you than all the other Greeks he ought to be destroyed? It is for you to show what view you take of those practices. If you condemn this man, you will declare your indignation at the things that have been done; but if you acquit him, you will be recognized as aspirants to the same conduct as theirs, and you will be unable to say that you are carrying out the injunctions of the Thirty, since nobody today is compelling you to vote against your judgment. So I counsel you not to condemn yourselves by acquitting them. Nor should you suppose that your voting is in secret for you will make your judgment manifest to the city.

You have heard, you have seen, you have suffered; you have them: give judgment.

LAW AGAINST SLANDER

[Editor's Note: The following speech "Against Theomnestos" (cited in Lysias 10: 6-9), was given in 384/3 B.C.. The speaker accuses Theomnestos of saying that the speaker had killed his own father during the time of the Thirty Tyrants circa 404 B.C. Athenian law evidently proscribed certain slanderous expressions ("forbidden words"): one was forbidden from calling another a "murderer." Theomnestos did not use that "forbidden word" but otherwise accused the speaker of killing his father. (The speaker had earlier claimed that Theomnestos threw away his shield and ran in battle.) The speaker asserts that the laws extended beyond those specific words to slanderous remarks in general.]

"But surely, men of the jury, you should go not by the words but by their sense, and you all know that those who have killed people are murderers and those who are murderers have killed people. It would have been a long business for the law-maker to write out all the words which have the same meaning; by mentioning one he indicates them all. You would not, I suppose, Theomnestos, demand legal satisfaction from someone who called you a father-beater or a mother-beater [forbidden words, it seems] and yet, if someone said that you hit your female parent or your male parent, think he should go unpunished because he had not said any of the forbidden words. I should like you to tell me this, since you are an expert on this subject and have made a practical and theoretical study of it: if someone said you had flung away your shield (when the law says 'if anyone alleges that he has thrown it away, he is to be liable to penalty'), would you refrain from bringing a case against him and be content to have flung away your shield, saying that it did not matter to you, because flinging is not the same as throwing?'"

LAWS AGAINST HYBRIS (HUBRIS)

[Editor's Note: The law against hybris (inadequately translated as arrogance: its full meaning connotes both energy and self-indulgence) is mentioned in a speech by Demosthenes, circa 340 B.C.:]

"If anyone treats with *hybris* any person, either child or woman or man, free or slave, or does anything illegal against any of these, let anyone who wishes, of those Athenians who are entitled, submit a *graphe* [charge, indictment] to the *thesmothetai* [appropriate magistrates]. Whoever [the court] finds guilty, let it immediately assess whatever penalty seems right for him to suffer or pay. Of those who submit private *graphai* , if anyone does not proceed, or when proceeding does not get 1/5 of the votes, let him pay 1000 drachmas to the public treasury. If a money penalty is assessed for the *hybris*, let the person be imprisoned, if the *hybris* is against a free person, until he pays it."

And

"So for *hybris* too the legislator allowed *graphai* to everyone who wishes, and made the penalty entirely payable to the state. He considered that a man who attempts to act with *hybris* wrongs the state, not just the victim; and that vengeance is sufficient compensation for the victim, and he ought not to take money for himself for such offences. And he went so far as to allow a *graphe* even for a slave, if anyone treats one with *hybris* . For he thought that what mattered was not the identity of the victim but the nature of the act; and since he found the act inexpedient, he did not allow it to be permitted either against a slave or at all. Nothing, men of Athens, nothing is more intolerable than *hybris* , or more deserving of your anger."

Also, from Aristotle, *Rhetoric* 1378b, 23-5):

"*Hybris* is doing and saying things at which the victim incurs dishonor, not in order to get for oneself anything which one did not get before, but so as to have pleasure."

LAWS AGAINST WRONGING THE ATHENIAN PEOPLE

[Editor's Note: Born in Athens, Xenophon (circa 430-355B.C.) was a disciple of Socrates and an admirer of Sparta. He served in the Spartan army that defeated Athens (394 B.C.) and Xenophon was subsequently banished from the city by the Athenians. Sparta rewarded him with an estate at Scillus, where he devoted himself to writing. Among his works was a continuation of the history of Thucydides (whose account ended in 410 B.C.). Xenophon took the story forward to 362 B.C.. Unlike Plato, who described Socrates as an unworldly philosopher, Xenophon emphasizes his mentor's pragmatic qualities. In the following document, Xenophon cites a decree proposed by Kannonos].

[The following document is from Xenophon's <u>Hellenica</u> I.7.20.:]

"If anyone wrongs the Athenian people, he is to make his defence in chains at a meeting of the people. If he is found guilty of doing wrong, he is to die and be thrown into the pit, and his property is to be confiscated and one-tenth of it is to belong to the Goddess."

Appendix C: Xenophon and Thucydides (Supplementary Texts)

XENOPHON, OECONOMICUS

Translated by E. C. Merchant (1923)

[Editor's Note: This dialogue was compiled by Xenophon. Like Plato, Xenophon was a student of Socrates. This dialogue provides some sense of ideal ethics and aesthetics of an Athenian nobleman. Here Socrates is seeking guidance from Ischomachus, "a gentleman."]

Socrates: So, happening one day to see him sitting in the cloister of the temple of Zeus Eleutherius apparently at leisure, I approached, and sitting down at his side, said:

"Why sitting still, Ischomachus? You are not much in the habit of doing nothing; for generally when I see you in the market-place you are either busy or at least not wholly idle."

"True, and you would not have seen me so now, Socrates, had I not made an appointment with some strangers here."

"Pray where do you spend your time,' said I, 'and what do you do when you are not engaged in some such occupation? For I want very much to learn how you came to be called a gentleman, since you do not pass your time indoors, and your condition does not suggest that you do so."

Smiling at my question, "How came you to be called a gentleman?", and apparently well pleased, Ischomachus answered: 'Well, Socrates, whether certain persons call me so when they talk to you about me, I know not. Assuredly when they challenge me to an exchange of property in order to escape some public burden, fitting a warship or providing a chorus, nobody looks for the   gentleman, but the challenge refers to me as plain Ischomachus, my father's son. Well now, Socrates, as you ask the question, I certainly do not pass my time indoors; for, you know, my wife is quite capable of looking after the house by herself."

"Ah, Ischomachus," said I, "that is just what I want to hear from you. Did you yourself train your wife to be of the right sort, or did she know her household duties when you received her from her parents?"

"Why, what knowledge could she have had, Socrates, when I took her for my wife? She was not yet fifteen years old when she came to me, and up to that time she had lived in leading-strings seeing, hearing and saying as little as possible. If when she came she knew no more than how, when given wool, to turn out a cloak, and had seen only how the spinning is given out to the maids, is not that as much as could be expected? For in control of her appetite, Socrates, she had been excellently trained; and this sort of training is, in my opinion the most important to man and woman alike."

"But in other respects did you train your wife yourself, Ischomachus, so that she should be competent to perform her duties?'

"Oh no, Socrates; not until I had first offered sacrifice and prayed that I might really teach, and she learn what was best for us both."

"Did not your wife join with you in these same sacrifices and prayers?"

"Oh yes, earnestly promising before heaven to behave as she ought to do; and it was easy to see that she would not neglect the lessons I taught her."

"Pray tell me, Ischomachus, what was the first lesson you taught her, since I would sooner hear this from your lips than an account of the noblest athletic event or horse-race?"

"Well, Socrates, as soon as I found her docile and sufficiently domesticated to carry on conversation, I questioned her to this effect:

"Tell me, dear, have you realised for what reason I took you and your parents gave you to me? For it is obvious to you, I am sure, that we should have had no difficulty in finding someone else to share our beds. But I for myself and your parents for you considered who was the best partner of home and children that we could get. My choice fell on you, and your parents, it appears, chose me as the best they could find. Now if God grants us children, we will then think out how we shall best train them. For one of the blessings in which we shall share is the acquisition of the very best of allies and the very best of support in old age; but at present we share in this our home. For I am paying into the common stock all that I have, and you have put in all that you brought with you. And we are not to reckon up which of us has actually contributed the greater amount, but we should know of a surety that the one who proves the better partner makes the more valuable contribution."

'My wife's answer was as follows, Socrates: How can I possibly help you? What power have I? Nay, all depends on you. My duty, as my mother told me, is to be discreet."

'Yes, of course, dear, I said, my father said the same to me. But discretion both in a man and a woman, means acting in such a manner that their possessions shall be in the best condition possible, and that as much as possible shall be added to them by fair and honourable means.

'And what do you see that I can possibly do to help in the improvement of our property? asked my wife.

'Why, said I, of course you must try to do as well as possible what the gods made you capable of doing and the law sanctions.

"And pray, what is that?" said she.

"Things of no small moment, I fancy, replied I, unless, indeed, the tasks over which the queen bee in the hive presides are of small moment. For it seems to me, dear, that the gods with great discernment have coupled together male and female, as they are called, chiefly in order that they may form a perfect partnership in mutual service. For, in the first place, that the various species of living creatures may not fail, they are joined in wedlock for the production of children. Secondly, offspring to support them in old age is provided by this union, to human beings, at any rate. Thirdly, human beings live not in the open air, like beasts, but obviously need shelter. Nevertheless, those who mean to win store to fill the covered place, have need of someone to work at the open-air occupations; since ploughing, sowing, planting and grazing are all such open-air employments; and these supply the needful food. Then again, as soon as this is stored in the covered place, then there is need of someone to keep it and to work at the things that must be done under cover. Cover is needed for the nursing of the infants; cover is needed for the making of the corn into bread, and likewise for the manufacture of clothes from the wool. And since both the indoor and the outdoor tasks demand labour and attention, God from the first adapted the woman's nature, I think, to the indoor and man's to the outdoor tasks and cares."

'For he made the man's body and mind more capable of enduring cold and heat, and journeys and campaigns; and therefore imposed on him the outdoor tasks. To the woman, since he has made her body less capable of such endurance, I take it that God has assigned the indoor tasks. And knowing that he had created in the woman and had imposed on her the nourishment of the infants, he meted out to her a larger portion of affection for new-born babes than to the man. And since he imposed on the woman the protection of the stores also, knowing that for protection a fearful disposition is no disadvantage, God meted out a larger share of fear to the woman than to the man; and knowing that he who deals with the outdoor tasks will have to be their defender against any wrong-doer, he meted out to him again a larger share of courage. But because both must give and take, he granted to both impartially memory and attention; and so you could not distinguish whether the male or the female sex has the larger share of these. And God also gave to both impartially the power to practise due self-control, and gave authority to whichever is the better—whether it be the man or the woman— to win a larger portion of the good that comes from it. And just because both have not the same aptitudes, they have the more need of each other, and each member of the pair is the more useful to the other, the one being competent where the other is deficient. ' Now since we know, dear, what duties have been assigned to each of us by God, we must endeavour, each of us, to do the duties allotted to us as well as possible. The law, moreover, approves of them, for it joins together man and woman. And as God has made them partners in their children, so the law appoints them partners in the home. And besides, the law declares those tasks to be honourable for each of them wherein God has made the one to excel the other. Thus, to the woman it is more honourable to stay indoors than to abide in the fields, but to the man it is unseemly rather to stay indoors than to attend to the work outside. If a man acts contrary to the nature God has given him, possibly his defiance is detected by the gods and he is punished for neglecting his own work, or meddling with his wife's. I think that the queen bee is busy about just such other tasks appointed by God."

' And pray,' said she, 'how do the queen bee's tasks resemble those that I have to do?'

' How? she stays in the hive, I answered, and does not suffer the bees to be idle; but those whose duty it is to work outside she sends forth to their work; and whatever each of them brings in, she knows and receives it, and keeps it till it is wanted. And when the time is come to use it, she portions out the just share to each. She likewise; presides over the weaving of the combs in the hive, that they may be well and quickly woven, and cares for the brood of little ones, that it be duly reared up. And when the young bees have been duly reared and are fit for work, she sends them forth to found a colony, with a leader to guide the young adventurers.

' Then shall I too have to do these things? said my wife.

' Indeed you will, said I; your duty will be to remain indoors and send out those servants whose work is outside, and superintend those who are to work indoors, and to receive the shopping goods, and distribute so much of them as must be spent, and watch over so much as is to be kept in store, and take care that the sum laid by for a year be not spent in a month. And when wool is brought to you, you must see that cloaks are made for those that want them. You must see too that the dry corn is in good condition for making food. One of the duties that fall to you, however, will perhaps seem rather thankless: you will have to see that any servant who is ill is cared for.

' Oh no, cried my wife, it will be delightful, assuming that those who are well cared for are going to feel grateful and be more loyal than before."

' Why, my dear, cried I, delighted with her answer, what makes the bees so devoted to their leader in the hive, that when she forsakes it, they all follow her, and not one thinks of staying behind? Is it not the result of some such thoughtful acts on her part?

' It would surprise me, answered my wife, if the leader's activities did not concern you more than me. For my care of the goods indoors and my management would look rather ridiculous, I fancy, if you did not see that something is gathered in from outside.

' And my ingathering would look ridiculous, I countered, if there were not someone to keep what is gathered in. Don't you see how they who 'draw water in a leaky jar,' as the saying goes, are pitied, because they seem to labour in vain?

' Of course, she said, for they are indeed in a miserable plight if they do that.

' But I assure you, dear, there are other duties peculiar to you that are pleasant to perform. It is delightful to teach spinning to a maid who had no knowledge of it when you received her, and to double her worth to you: to take in hand a girl who is ignorant of housekeeping and service, and after teaching her and making her trustworthy and serviceable to find her worth any amount: to have the power of rewarding the discreet and useful members of your household, and of punishing anyone who turns out to be a rogue. But the pleasantest experience of all is to prove yourself better than I am, to make me your servant; and, so far from having cause to fear that as you grow older you may be less honored in the household, to feel confident that with advancing years, the better partner you prove to me and the better housewife to our children, the greater will be the honor paid to you in our home. For it is not through outward comeliness that the sum of things good and beautiful is increased in the world, but by the daily practice of the virtues."

'Such was the tenor of my earliest talks with her, Socrates, so far as I can recall them.'

Book 8.. 'And did you find, Ischomachus, that they acted as a stimulus to her diligence?' I asked.

'Yes, indeed,' answered Ischomachus, 'and I recollect that she was vexed and blushed crimson, because she could not give me something from the stores when I asked for it. And seeing that she was annoyed, I said: Don't worry, dear, because you cannot give me what I am asking for. For not to be able to use a thing when you want it is poverty unquestionably; but failure to get the thing that you seek is less grievous than not to seek it at all because you know that it does not exist. The fact is, you are not to blame for this, but I, because I handed over the things to you without giving directions where they were to be put, so that you might know where to put them and where to find them. My dear, there is nothing so convenient or so good for human beings as order. Thus, a chorus is a combination of human beings; but when the members of it do as they choose, it becomes mere confusion, and there is no pleasure in watching it; but when they act and chant in an orderly fashion, then those same men at once seem worth seeing and worth hearing. Again, my dear, an army in disorder is a confused mass, an easy prey to enemies, a disgusting sight to friends and utterly useless,— donkey, trooper, carrier, light-armed, horseman, chariot, huddled together. For how are they to march in such a plight, when they hamper one another, some walking while others run, some running while others halt, chariot colliding with horseman, donkey with chariot, carrier with trooper? If there is fighting to be done, how can they fight in such a state? For the units that must needs run away when attacked are enough to trample underfoot the heavy infantry. But an army in orderly array is a noble sight to friends, and an unwelcome spectacle to the enemy. What friend would not rejoice as he watches a strong body of troopers marching in order, would not admire cavalry riding in squadrons? And what enemy would not fear troopers, horsemen, light-armed, archers, slingers disposed in serried ranks and following their officers in orderly fashion? Nay, even on the march where order is kept, though they number tens of thousands, all move steadily forward as one man; for the line behind is continually filling up the gap. Or, again, why is a: man-of-war laden with men terrible to an enemy and a goodly sight to friends, if not for its speed? Why do the men on board not hamper one another? Is it not just because they are seated in order, swing forward and backward in order, embark and disembark in order? If I want a type of disorder, I think of a farmer who has stored barley, wheat and pulse in one bin; and then when he wants a bannock or a loaf or a pudding, must pick out the grain instead of finding it separate and ready for use.

' And so, my dear, if you do not want this confusion, and wish to know exactly how to manage our goods, and to find with ease whatever is wanted, and to satisfy me by giving me anything I ask for, let us choose the place that each portion should occupy; and, having put the things in their place, let us instruct the maid to take them from it and put them back again. Thus we shall know what is safe and sound and what is not; for the place itself will miss whatever is not in it, and a glance will reveal anything that wants attention, and the knowledge where each thing is will quickly bring it to hand, so that we can use it without trouble.

'Once I had an opportunity of looking over the great Phoenician merchantman, Socrates, and I thought I had never seen tackle so excellently and accurately arranged. For I never saw so many bits of stuff packed away separately in so small a receptacle. As you know, a ship needs a great quantity of wooden and corded implements when she comes into port or puts to sea, much rigging, as it is called, when she sails, many contrivances to protect her against enemy vessels; she carries a large supply of arms for the men, and contains a set of household utensils for each mess. In addition to all this, she is laden with cargo which the skipper carries for profit. And all the things I mention were contained in a chamber of little more than a hundred square cubits. And I noticed that each kind of thing was so neatly stowed away that there was no confusion, no work for a searcher, nothing out of place, no troublesome untying to cause delay when anything was wanted for immediate use. I found that the steersman's servant, who is called the mate, knows each particular section so exactly, that he can tell even when away where everything is kept and how much there is of it, just as well as a man who knows how to spell can tell how many letters there are in Socrates and in what order they come. Now I saw this man in his spare time inspecting all the stores that are wanted, as a matter of course, in the ship. I was surprised to see him looking over them, and asked what he was doing. Sir, he answered, I am looking to see how the ship's tackle is stored, in case of accident, or whether anything is missing or mixed up with other stuff. For when God sends a storm at sea, there's no time to search about for what you want or to serve it out if it's in a muddle. For God threatens and punishes careless fellows, and you're lucky if he merely refrains from destroying the innocent; and if he saves you when you do your work well, you have much cause to thank heaven.

'Now after seeing the ship's tackle in such perfect order, I told my wife: Considering that folk aboard a merchant vessel, even though it be a little one, find room for things and keep order, though tossed violently to and fro, and find what they want to get, though terror-stricken, it would be downright carelessness on our part if we, who have large storerooms in our house to keep everything separate and whose house rests on solid ground, fail to find a good and handy place for everything. Would it not be sheer stupidity on our part?

' How good it is to keep one's stock of utensils in order, and how easy to find a suitable place in a house to put each set in, I have already said. And what a beautiful sight is afforded by boots of all sorts and conditions ranged in rows! How beautiful it is to see cloaks of all sorts and conditions kept separate, or blankets, or brazen vessels, or table furniture! Yes, no serious man will smile when I claim that there is beauty in the order even of pots and pans set out in neat array, however much it may move the laughter of a wit. There is nothing, in short, that does not gain in beauty when set out in order. For each set looks like a troop of utensils, and the space between the sets is beautiful to see, when each set is kept clear of it, just as a troop of dancers about the altar is a beautiful spectacle in itself, and even the free space looks beautiful and unencumbered.

' We can test the truth of what I say, dear, without any inconvenience and with very little trouble. Moreover, my dear, there is no ground for any misgiving that it is hard to find someone who will get to know the various places and remember to put each set in its proper place. For we know, I take it, that the city as a whole has ten thousand times as much of everything as we have; and yet you may order any sort of servant to buy something in the market and to bring it home, and he will be at no loss: every one of them is bound to know where he should go to get each article. Now the only reason for this is that everything is kept in a fixed place. But when you are searching for a person, you often fail to find him, though he may be searching for you himself. And for this again the one reason is that no place of meeting has been fixed.

'Such is the gist of the conversation I think I remember having with her about the arrangement of utensils and their use.'

Book 9. 'And what was the result?' I asked; 'did you think, Ischomachus, that your wife paid any heed to the lessons you tried so earnestly to teach her?'

' Why, she promised to attend to them, and was evidently pleased beyond measure to feel that she had found a solution of her difficulties, and she begged me to lose no time in arranging things as I had suggested.

'And how did you arrange things for her, Ischomachus?' I asked.

'Why, I decided first to show her the possibilities of our house. For it contains few elaborate decorations, Socrates; but the rooms are designed simply with the object of providing as convenient receptacles as possible for the things that are to fill them, and thus each room invited just what was suited to it. Thus the store-room by the security of its I position called for the most valuable blankets and utensils, the dry covered rooms for the corn, the cool for the wine, the well-lit for those works of art and vessels that need light. I showed her decorated living-rooms for the family that are cool in summer and warm in winter. I showed her that the whole house fronts south, so that it was obvious that it is sunny in winter and shady in summer. I showed her the women's quarters too, separated by a bolted door from the men's, so that nothing which ought not to be moved may be taken out, and that the servants may not breed without our leave. For honest servants generally prove more loyal if they have a family; but rogues, if they live in wedlock, become all the more prone to mischief.

'And now that we had completed the list, we forthwith set about separating the furniture tribe by tribe. We began by collecting together the vessels we use in sacrificing. After that we put together the women's holiday finery, and the men's holiday and war garb, blankets in the women's, blankets in the men's quarters, women's shoes, men's shoes. Another tribe consisted of arms, and three others of implements for spinning, for bread-making and for cooking; others, again, of the tilings required for washing, at the kneading-trough, and for table use. All these we divided into two sets, things in constant use and things reserved for festivities. We also put by themselves the things consumed month by month, and set apart the supplies calculated to last for a year. For this plan makes it easier to tell how they will last to the end of the time. When we had divided all the portable property tribe by tribe, we arranged everything in its proper place. After that we showed the servants who have to use them where to keep the utensils they require daily, for baking, cooking, spinning and so forth; handed them over to their care and charged them to see that they were safe and sound. The things that we use only for festivals or entertainments, or on rare occasions, we handed over to the housekeeper, and after showing her their places and counting and making a written list of all the items, we told her to give them out to the right servants, to remember what she gave to each of them, and when receiving them back to put everything in the place from which she took it.

'In appointing the housekeeper, we chose the woman whom on consideration we judged to be the most temperate in eating and wine drinking and sleeping and the most modest with men, the one, too, who seemed to have the best memory, to be most careful not to offend us by neglecting her duties, and to think most how she could earn some reward by obliging us. We also taught her to be loyal to us by making her a partner in all our joys and calling on her to share our troubles. Moreover, we trained her to be eager for the improvement of our estate, by making her familiar with it and by allowing her to share in our success. And further, we put justice into her, by giving more honour to the just than to the unjust, and by showing her that the just live in greater wealth and freedom than the unjust; and we placed her in that position of superiority.

'When all this was done, Socrates, I told my wife that all these measures were futile, unless she saw to it herself that our arrangement was strictly adhered to in every detail. I explained that in well-ordered cities the citizens are not satisfied with passing good laws: they go further, and choose guardians of the laws, who act as overseers, commending the law-abiding and punishing law-breakers. So I charged my wife to consider herself guardian of the laws to our household. And just as the commander of a garrison inspects his guards, so must she inspect the chattels whenever she thought it well to do so; as the Council scrutinises the cavalry and the horses, so she was to make sure that everything was in good condition: like a queen, she must reward the worthy with praise and honor, so far as in her lay, and not spare rebuke and punishment when they were called for.

' Moreover, I taught her that she should not be vexed that I assigned heavier duties to her than to the servants in respect of our possessions. Servants, I pointed out, carry, tend and guard their master's property, and only in this sense have a share in it; they have no right to use anything except by the owner's leave; but everything belongs to the master, to use it as he will. Therefore, I explained, he who gains most by the preservation of the goods and loses most by their destruction, is the one who is bound to take most care of them.'most care of them.'

'Well, now, Ischornachus,' said I, ' was your wife inclined to pay heed to your words?'

'Why, Socrates,' he cried, 'she just told me that I was mistaken if I supposed that I was laying a hard task on her in telling her that she must take care of our things. It would have been harder, she said, had I required her to neglect her own possessions, than to have the duty of attending to her own peculiar blessings. The fact is,' he added, 'just as it naturally comes easier to a good woman to care for her own children than to neglect them, so, I imagine, a good woman finds it pleasanter to look after her own possessions than to neglect them.'

Book 10. Now when I heard that his wife had given him this answer, I exclaimed; ' Upon my word, Ischomachus, your wife has a truly masculine mind by your showing!'

'Yes,' said Ischomachus, 'and I am prepared to give you other examples of high-mindedness on her part, when a word from me was enough to secure her instant obedience.'

'Tell me what they are,' I cried; 'for if Zeuxis showed me a fair woman's portrait painted by his own hand, it would not give me half the pleasure I derive from the contemplation of a living woman's virtues.'

Thereupon Ischomachus took up his parable. 'Well, one day, Socrates, I noticed that her face was made up: she had rubbed in white lead in order to look even whiter than she is, and alkanet juice to heighten the rosy color of her cheeks; and she was wearing boots with thick soles to increase her height. So I said to her, Tell me, my dear, how should I appear more worthy of your love as a partner in our goods, by disclosing to you our belongings just as they are, without boasting of imaginary possessions or concealing any part of what we have, or by trying to trick you with an exaggerated account, showing you bad money and gilt necklaces and describing clothes that will fade as real purple?

' Hush! she broke in immediately, pray don't be like that—I could not love you with all my heart if you were like that!

' Then, are we not joined together by another bond of union, dear, to be partners in our bodies?

' The world says so, at any rate.

' How then should I seem more worthy of your love in this partnership of the body—by striving to have my body hale and strong when I present it to you, and so literally to be of a good countenance in your sight, or by smearing my cheeks with red lead and painting myself under the eyes with rouge before I show myself to you and clasp you in my arms, cheating you and offering to your eyes and hands red lead instead of my real flesh?

' Oh, she cried, I would sooner touch you than red lead, would sooner see your own color than rouge, would sooner see your eyes bright than smeared with grease."

' Then please assume, my dear, that I do not prefer white paint and dye of alkanet to your real color; but just as the gods have made horses to delight in horses, cattle in cattle, sheep in sheep, so human beings find the human body undisguised most delightful. Tricks like these may serve to gull outsiders, but people who live together are bound to be found out, if they try to deceive one another. For they are found out while they are dressing in the morning; they perspire and are lost; a tear convicts them; the bath reveals them as they are!'

'And, pray, what did she say to that?' I asked.

'Nothing,' he said, 'only she gave up such practices from that day forward, and tried to let me see her undisguised and as she should be. Still, she did ask whether I could advise her on one point: how she might make herself really beautiful, instead of merely seeming to be so. And this was my advice, Socrates: Don't sit about for ever like a slave, but try, God helping you, to behave as a mistress: stand before the loom and be ready to instruct those who know less than you, and to learn from those who know more: look after the baking-maid: stand by the housekeeper when she is serving out stores: go round and see whether everything is in its place. For I thought that would give her a walk as well as occupation. I also said it was excellent exercise to mix flour and knead dough; and to shake and fold cloaks and bedclothes; such exercise would give her a better appetite, improve her health, and add natural colour to her cheeks. Besides, when a wife's looks outshine a maid's, and she is fresher and more becomingly dressed, they're a ravishing sight, especially when the wife is also willing to oblige, whereas the girl's services are compulsory. But wives who sit about like fine ladies, expose themselves to comparison with painted and fraudulent hussies. And now, Socrates, you may be sure, my wife's dress and appearance are in accord with my instructions and with my present description.'

Book 11. At this point I said, 'Ischomachus, I think your account of your wife's occupations is sufficient for the present—and very creditable it is to both of you. But now tell me of your own: thus you will have the satisfaction of stating the reasons why you are so highly respected, and I shall be much beholden to you for a complete account of a gentleman's occupations, and if my understanding serves, for a thorough knowledge of them.'

'Well then, Socrates,' answered Ischomachus, 'it will be a very great pleasure to me to give you an account of my daily occupations, that you may correct me if you think there is anything amiss in my conduct.'

'As to that,' said I, ' how could I presume to correct a perfect gentleman, I who am supposed to be a mere chatterer with my head in the air, I who am called—the most senseless of all taunts—a poor beggar? I do assure you, Ischomachus, this last imputation would have driven me to despair, were it not that a day or two ago I came upon the horse of Nicias the foreigner. I saw a crowd walking behind the creature and staring, and heard some of them talking volubly about him. Well, I went up to the groom and asked him if the horse had many possessions. The man looked at me as if I must be mad to ask such a question, and asked me how a horse could own property. At that I recovered, for his answer showed that it is possible even for a poor horse to be a good one, if nature has given him a good spirit. Assume, therefore, that it is possible for me to be a good man, and give me a complete account of your occupations, that, so far as my understanding allows me, I may endeavor to follow your example from to-morrow morning; for that's a good day for entering on a course of virtue.'

'You're joking, Socrates,' said Ischomachus; 'nevertheless I will tell you what principles I try my best to follow consistently in life. For I seem to realize that, while the gods have made it impossible for men to prosper without knowing and attending to the things they ought to do, to some of the wise and careful they grant prosperity, and to some deny it; and therefore I begin by worshipping the gods, and try to conduct myself in such a way that I may have health and strength in answer to my prayers, the respect of my fellow-citizens, the affection of my friends, safety with honor in war, and wealth increased by honest means.'

'What, Ischomachus,' I asked on hearing that, 'do you really want to be rich and to have much, along with much trouble to take care of it?'

'The answer to your questions,' said he, 'is, Yes, I do indeed. For I would fain honor the gods without counting the cost, Socrates, help friends in need, and look to it that the city lacks no adornment that my means can supply.'

'Truly noble aspirations, Ischomachus,' I cried 'and worthy of a man of means, no doubt! Seeing that there are many who cannot live without help from others, and many are content if they can get enough for their own needs, surely those who can maintain their own estate and yet have enough left to adorn the city and relieve their friends may well be thought high and mighty men. However,' I added, 'praise of such men is a commonplace among us. Please return to your first statement, Ischomachus, and tell me how you take care of your health and your strength, how you make it possible to come through war with safety and honor. I shall be content to hear about your money-making afterwards.'

'Well, Socrates,' replied Ischomachus, 'all these things hang together, so far as I can see. For if a man has plenty to eat, and works off the effects properly, I take it that he both insures his health and adds to his strength. By training himself in the arts of war he is more qualified to save himself honorably, and by due diligence and avoidance of loose habits, he is more likely to increase his estate.'

'So far, Ischomachus, I follow you,' I answered. 'You mean that by working after meals, by diligence and by training, a man is more apt to obtain the good things of life. But now I should like you to give me details. By what kind of work do you endeavor to keep your health and strength? How do you train yourself in the arts of war? What diligence do you use to have a surplus from which to help friends and strengthen the city?'

'Well now, Socrates,' replied Ischomachus, 'I rise from my bed at an hour when, if I want to call on anyone, I am sure to find him still at home. If I have any business to do in town, I make it an opportunity for getting a walk. If there is nothing pressing to be done in town, my servant leads my horse to the farm, and I make my walk by going to it on foot, with more benefit, perhaps, Socrates, than if I took a turn in the arcade. When I reach the farm, I may find planting, clearing, sowing or harvesting in progress. I superintend all the details of the work, and make any improvements in method that I can suggest. After this, I usually mount my horse and go through exercises, imitating as closely as I can the exercises needed in warfare. I avoid neither slope nor steep incline, ditch nor watercourse, but I use all possible care not to lame my horse when he takes them. After I have finished, the servant gives the horse a roll and leads him home, bringing with him from the farm anything we happen to want in the city. I divide the return home between walking and running. Arrived, I clean myself with a strigil [stick for scraping sweat], and then I have lunch, Socrates, eating just enough to get through the day neither empty-bellied nor too full.'

'Upon my word, Ischomachus,' cried I, 'I am delighted with your activities. For you have a pack of appliances for securing health and strength, of exercises for war and specifics for getting rich, and you use them all at the same time! That does seem to me admirable! And in fact you afford convincing proofs that your method in pursuing each of these objects is sound. For we see you generally in the enjoyment of health and strength, thanks to the gods, and we know that you are considered one of our best horsemen and wealthiest citizens.'

'And what comes of these activities, Socrates? Not, as you perhaps expected to hear, that I am generally dubbed a gentleman, but that I am persistently slandered.'

'Ah,' said I, 'but I was meaning to ask you, Ischomachus, whether you include in your system ability to conduct a prosecution and defense, in case you have to appear in the courts?'

'Why, Socrates,' he answered, 'do you not see that this is just what I am constantly practicing— showing my traducers that I wrong no man and do all the good I can to many? And do you not think that I practice myself in accusing, by taking careful note of certain persons who are doing wrong to many individuals and to the state, and are doing no good to anyone?'

'But tell me one thing more, Ischomachus,' I said; 'do you also practice the art of expounding these matters?'

'Why, Socrates,' he replied, 'I assiduously practice the art of speaking. For I get one of the servants to act as prosecutor or defendant, and try to confute him; or I praise or blame someone before his friends; or I act as peace-maker between some of my acquaintances by trying to show them that it is to their interest to be friends rather than enemies. I assist at a court-martial and censure a soldier, or take turns in defending a man who is unjustly blamed, or in accusing one who is unjustly honored. We often sit in counsel and speak in support of the course we want to adopt and against the course we want to avoid. I have often been singled out before now, Socrates, and condemned to suffer punishment or pay damages.'

'By whom, Ischomachus? 'I asked; 'I am in the dark about that!'

'By my wife,' was his answer.

'And, pray, how do you plead?' said I.

'Pretty well, when it is to my interest to speak the truth. But when lying is called for, Socrates, I can't make the worse cause appear the better—oh no, not at all.'

'Perhaps, Ischomachus,' I commented, 'you can't make the falsehood into the truth!'

Book 12. 'But perhaps I am keeping you, Ischomachus,' I continued, 'and you want to get away now?'

'Oh no, Socrates, he answered;' I should not think of going before the market empties.'

'To be sure,' I continued; 'you take the utmost care not to forfeit your right to be called a gentleman! For I daresay there are many things claiming your attention now; but, as you have made an appointment with those strangers, you are determined not to break it.'

'But I assure you, Socrates, I am not neglecting the matters you refer to, either; for I keep bailiffs on my farms.'

'And when you want a bailiff, Ischomachus, do you look out for a man qualified for such a post, and then try to buy him—when you want a builder, I feel sure you inquire for a qualified man and try to get him—or do you train your bailiffs yourself?'

'Of course I try to train them myself, Socrates. For the man has to be capable of taking charge in my absence; so why need he know anything but what I know myself? For if I am fit to manage the farm, I presume I can teach another man what I know myself.'

' Then the first requirement will be that he should be loyal to you and yours, if he is to represent you in your absence. For if a steward is not loyal, what is the good of any knowledge he may possess?'

'None, of course; but I may tell you, loyalty to me and to mine is the first lesson I try to teach.'

'And how, in heaven's name, do you teach your man to be loyal to you and yours?'

'By rewarding him, of course, whenever the gods bestow some good thing on us in abundance.'

'You mean, then, that those who enjoy a share of your good things are loyal to you and want you to prosper?'

'Yes, Socrates, I find that is the best instrument for producing loyalty.'

'But, now, if he is loyal to you, Ischomachus, will that be enough to make him a competent bailiff? Don't you see that though all men, practically, wish themselves well, yet there are many who won't take the trouble to get for themselves the good things they want to have?'

'Well, when I want to make bailiffs of such men, of course I teach them also to be careful.'

'Pray how do you do that? I was under the impression that carefulness is a virtue that can't possibly he taught.'

'True, Socrates, it isn't possible to teach everyone you come across to be careful.'

'Very well; what sort of men can be taught? Point these out to me, at all events.'

'In the first place, Socrates, you can't make careful men of hard drinkers; for drink makes them forget everything they ought to do.'

'Then are drunkards the only men who will never become careful, or are there others?'

'Of course there are--sluggards must be included; for you can't do your own business when you are asleep, nor make others do theirs.'

'Well then, will these make up the total of persons incapable of learning this lesson, or are there yet others besides?'

'I should add that in my opinion a man who falls desperately in love is incapable of giving more attention to anything than he gives to the object of his passion. For it isn't easy to find hope or occupation more delightful than devotion to the darling! aye, and when the thing to be done presses, no harder punishment can easily be thought of than the prevention of intercourse with the beloved! Therefore I shrink from attempting to make a manager of that sort of man too.'

'And what about the men who have a passion for lucre? Are they also incapable of being trained to take charge of the work of a farm?'

'Not at all; of course not. In fact, they very easily qualify for the work. It is merely necessary to point out to them that diligence is profitable.'

'And assuming that the others are free from the faults that you condemn and are covetous of gain in a moderate degree, how do you teach them to be careful in the affairs you want them to superintend?'

'By a very simple plan, Socrates. Whenever I notice that they are careful, I commend them and try to show them honour; but when they appear careless, I try to say and do the sort of things that will sting them.'

'Turn now, Ischomachus, from the subject of the men in training for the occupation, and tell me about the system: is it possible for anyone to make others careful if he is careless himself?'

'Of course not: an unmusical person could as soon teach music. For it is hard to learn to do a thing well when the teacher prompts you badly; and when a master prompts a servant to be careless, it is difficult for the man to become a good servant. To put it shortly, I don't think I have discovered a bad master with good servants: I have, however, come across a good master with bad servants—but they suffered for it! If you want to make men fit to take charge, you must supervise their work and examine it, and be ready to reward work well carried through, and not shrink from punishing carelessness as it deserves. I like the answer that is attributed to the Persian. The king, you know, had happened on a good horse, and wanted to fatten him as speedily as possible. So he asked one who was reputed clever with horses what is the quickest way of fattening a horse. The master's eye, replied the man. I think we may apply the answer generally, Socrates, and say that the master's eye in the main does the good and worthy work.'

Book 13. 'When you have impressed on a man, I resumed, 'the necessity of careful attention to the duties you assign to him, will he then be competent to act as bailiff, or must he learn something besides, if he is to be efficient?'

'Of course,' answered Ischomachus, 'he has still to understand what he has to do, and when and how to do it. Otherwise how could a bailiff be of more use than a doctor who takes care to visit a patient early and late, but has no notion of the right way to treat his illness?'

'Well, but suppose he has learned how farm-work is to be done, will he want something more yet, or will your man now be a perfect bailiff ?'

'I think he must learn to rule the laborers.'

'And do you train your bailiffs to be competent to rule too ?'

'Yes, I try, anyhow.

'And pray tell me how you train them to be rulers of men.'

'By a childishly easy method, Socrates. I daresay you'll laugh if I tell you.'

'Oh, but it is certainly not a laughing matter, Ischomachus. For anyone who can make men fit to rule others can also teach them to be masters of others; and if he can make them fit to be masters, he can make them fit to be kings. So anyone who can do that seems to me to deserve high praise rather than laughter.'

'Well now, Socrates, other creatures learn obedience in two ways—by being punished when they try to disobey, and by being rewarded when they are eager to serve you. Colts, for example, learn to obey the horsebreaker by getting something they like when they are obedient, and suffering inconvenience when they are disobedient, until they carry out the horsebreaker's intentions. Puppies, again, are much inferior to men in intelligence and power of expression; and yet they learn to run in circles and turn somersaults and do many other tricks in the same way; for when they obey they get something that they want, and when they are careless, they are punished. And men can be made more obedient by word of mouth merely, by being-shown that it is good for them to obey. But in dealing with slaves the training thought suitable for wild animals is also a very effective way of teaching obedience; for you will do much with them by filling their bellies with the food they hanker after. Those of an ambitious disposition are also spurred on by praise, some natures being hungry for praise as others for meat and drink. Now these are precisely the things that I do myself with a view to making men more obedient; but they are not the only lessons I give to those whom I want to appoint my bailiffs. I have other ways of helping them on. For the clothes that I must provide for my workpeople and the shoes are not all alike. Some are better than others, some worse, in order that I may reward the better servant with the superior articles, and give the inferior things to the less deserving. For I think it is very disheartening to good servants, Socrates, when they see that they do all the work, and others who are not willing to work hard and run risks when need be, get the same as they. For my part, then, I don't choose to put the deserving on a level with the worthless, and when I know that my bailiffs have distributed the best things to the most deserving, I commend them; and if I see that flattery or any other futile service wins special favor, I don't overlook it, but reprove the bailiff, and try to show him, Socrates, that such favoritism is not even in his own interest.'

Book 14. 'Now, Ischomachus,' said I, 'when you find your man so competent to rule that he can make them obedient, do you think him a perfect bailiff, or does he want anything else, even with the qualifications you have mentioned?'

'Of course, Socrates,' returned Ischomachus, ' he must be honest and not touch his master's property. For if the man who handles the crops dares to make away with them, and doesn't leave enough to give a profit on the undertaking, what good can come of farming under his management?'

'Then do you take it on yourself to teach this kind of justice too ?'

'Certainly: I don't find, however, that all readily pay heed to this lesson. Nevertheless I guide the servants into the path of justice with the aid of maxims drawn from the laws of Draco and Solon. For it seems to me that these famous men enacted many of their laws with an eye on this particular kind of justice. For it is written: thieves shall be fined for their thefts, and anyone guilty of attempt shall be imprisoned if taken in the act, and put to death. The object of these enactments was clearly to make covetousness unprofitable to the offender. By applying some of these clauses and other enactments found in the Persian king's code, I try to make my servants upright in the matters that pass through their hands. For while those laws only penalise the wrongdoer, the king's code not only punishes the guilty, but also benefits the upright. Thus, seeing that the honest grow richer than the dishonest, many, despite their love of lucre, are careful to remain free from dishonesty. And if I find any attempting to persist in dishonesty, although they are well treated, I regard them as incorrigibly greedy, and have nothing more to do with them. On the other hand, if I discover that a man is inclined to be honest not only because he gains by his honesty, but also from a desire to win my approbation, I treat him like a free man by making him rich; and not only so, but I honour him as a gentleman. For I think, Socrates, that the difference between ambition and greed consists in this, that for the sake of praise and honor the ambitious are willing to work properly, to take risks and refrain from dishonest gain.'

Book 15. 'Well, well, I won't go on to ask whether anything more is wanting to your man, after you have implanted in him a desire for your prosperity and have made him also careful to see that you achieve it, and have obtained for him, besides, the knowledge needful to ensure that every piece of work done shall add to the profits, and, further, have made him capable of ruling, and when, besides all this, he takes as much delight in producing heavy crops for you in due season as you would take if you did the work yourself. For it seems to me that a man like that would make a very valuable bailiff. Nevertheless, Ischomachus, don't leave a gap in that part of the subject to which we have given the most cursory attention.'

'Which is it?' asked Ischomachus.

'You said, you know, that the greatest lesson to learn is how things ought to be done; and added that, if a man is ignorant what to do and how to do it, no good can come of his management.

Then he said, 'Socrates, are you insisting now that I should teach the whole art and mystery of agriculture?'

'Yes,' said I; 'for maybe it is just this that makes rich men of those who understand it, and condemns the ignorant to a life of penury, for all their toil.'

'Well, Socrates, you shall now hear how kindly a thing is this art. Helpful, pleasant, honorable, dear to gods and men in the highest degree, it is also in the highest degree easy to learn. Noble qualities surely! As you know, we call those creatures noble that are beautiful, great and helpful, and yet gentle towards men.

'Ah, but I think, Ischomachus, that I quite understand your account of these matters—I mean how to teach a bailiff; for I think I follow your statement that you make him loyal to you, and careful and capable of ruling and honest. But you said that one who is to be successful in the management of a farm must learn what to do and how and when to do it. That is the subject that we have treated, it seems to me, in a rather cursory fashion, as if you said that anyone who is to be capable of writing from dictation and reading what is written must know the alphabet. For had I been told that, I should have been told, to be sure, that I must know the alphabet, but I don't think that piece of information would help me to know it. So too now; I am easily convinced that a man who is to manage a farm successfully must understand farming, but that knowledge doesn't help me to understand how to farm. Were I to decide this very moment to be a farmer, I think I should be like that doctor who goes round visiting the sick, but has no knowledge of the right way to treat them. Therefore, that I may not be like him, you must teach me the actual operations of farming.'

'Why, Socrates, farming is not troublesome to learn, like other arts, which the pupil must study till he is worn out before he can earn his keep by his work. Some things you can understand by watching men at work, others by just being told, well enough to teach another if you wish. And I believe that you know a good deal about it yourself, without being aware of the fact. The truth is that, whereas other artists conceal more or less the most important points in their own art, the farmer who plants best is most pleased when he is being watched, so is he who sows best. Question him about any piece of work well done: and he will tell you exactly how he did it. So farming, Socrates, more than any other calling, seems to produce a generous disposition in its followers.'

'An excellent preamble,' I cried, 'and not of a sort to damp the weaver's curiosity. Come, describe it to me, all the more because it is so simple to learn. For it is no disgrace to you to teach elementary lessons, but far more a disgrace to me not to understand them, especially if they are really useful.'

Book 16. 'First then, Socrates, I want to show you that what is called the most complicated problem in agriculture by the authors who write most accurately on the theory of the subject, but are not practical farmers, is really a simple matter. For they tell us that to be a successful farmer one must first know the nature of the soil.'

'Yes, and they are right,' I remarked; 'for if you don't know what the soil is capable of growing, you can't know, I suppose, what to plant or what to sow.'

'Well then,' said Ischomachus, 'you can tell by looking at the crops and trees on another man's land what the soil can and what it cannot grow. But when you have found out, it is useless to fight against the gods. For you are not likely to get a better yield from the land by sowing and planting what you want instead of the crops and trees that the land prefers. If it happens that the land does not declare its own capabilities because the owners are lazy, you can often gather more correct information from a neighboring plot than from a neighboring proprietor. Yes, and even if the land lies waste, it reveals its nature. For if the wild stuff growing on the land is of fine quality, then by good farming the soil is capable of yielding cultivated crops of fine quality. So the nature of the soil can be ascertained even by the novice who has no experience of farming.'

'Well, I think I am now confident, Ischomachus, that I need not avoid farming from fear of not knowing the nature of the soil. The fact is, I am reminded that fishermen, though their business is in the sea, and they neither stop the boat to take a look nor slow down, nevertheless, when they see the crops as they scud past the farms, do not hesitate to express an opinion about the land, which is the good and which is the bad sort, now condemning, now praising it. And, what is more, I notice that in their opinion about the good land they generally agree exactly with experienced farmers.'

'Then, Socrates, let me refresh your memory on the subject of agriculture; but where do you wish me to begin? For I am aware that I shall tell you very much that you know already about the right method of farming.'

'First, Ischomachus, I think I should be glad to learn, for this is the philosopher's way, how I am to cultivate the land if I want to get the heaviest crops of wheat and barley out of it.'

' Well, you know, I take it, that fallow must be prepared for sowing?'

' Yes, I know.'

'Suppose, then, we start ploughing in winter?'

'Why, the land will be a bog!'

'How about starting in summer? '

'The land will be hard to plough up.'

'It seems that spring is the season for beginning this work.'

'Yes, the land is likely to be more friable if it is broken up then.'

'Yes, and the grass turned up is long enough at that season to serve as manure, but, not having shed seed, it will not grow. You know also, I presume, that fallow land can't be satisfactory unless it is clear of weeds and thoroughly baked in the sun?'

'"Yes, certainly; that is essential, I think.'

'Do you think that there is any better way of securing that than by turning the land over as often as possible in summer?'

'Nay, I know for certain that if you want the weeds to lie on the surface and wither in the heat, and the land to be baked by the sun, the surest way is to plough it up at midday in midsummer.'

'And if men prepare the fallow by digging, is it not obvious that they too must separate the weeds from the soil?'

'Yes, and they must throw the weeds on the surface to wither, and turn up the ground so that the lower spit may be baked.'

Book 17. ' You see, then, Socrates, that we agree about the fallow.'

'It does seem so, to be sure.'

'And now as to the time for sowing, Socrates. Is it not your opinion that the time to sow is that which has been invariably found to be the best by past experience, and is universally approved by present practice? For as soon as autumn ends, all men, I suppose, look anxiously to God, to see when he will send rain on the earth and make them free to sow.'

'Yes, Ischomachus, all men have made up their minds, of course, not to sow in dry ground if they can help it, those who sowed without waiting to be bidden by God having had to wrestle with many losses.'

'So far, then,' said Ischomachus, 'all the world is of one mind.'

'Yes,' said I, ' where God is our teacher we all come to think alike. For example, all agree that it is better to wear warm clothes in winter, if they can, and all agree on the desirability of having a fire, if they have wood.'

'But,' said Ischomachus, ' when we come to the question whether sowing is best done early or very late or at the mid-season, we find much difference of opinion, Socrates.

'And God, said I, 'does not regulate the year by fixed laws; but in one year it may be advantageous to sow early, in another very late, in another at mid-season.'

'Then do you think, Socrates, that it is better to select one of these times for sowing, whether you sow much or little, or to begin at the earliest moment and continue sowing to the latest?'

'For my part, Ischomachus, I think it is best to sow for succession throughout the season. For in my opinion it is much better to get enough food at all times than too much at one time and not enough at another.'

'Here again, then, Socrates, pupil and teacher are of one opinion; and, moreover, you, the pupil, are first in stating this opinion.'

'Well now, is casting the seed a complicated problem?'

'By all means let us take that also into consideration, Socrates. I presume that you know as well as I that the seed must be cast by the hand ? '

'Yes, I have seen it.'

'Ah,' he said, 'but some men can cast evenly, and some cannot.'

'Then sowers no less than lyre-players need practice, that the hand may be the servant of the will.'

'Certainly. But suppose that some of the land is rather light and some rather heavy ?'

'What do you mean by that?' I interrupted. By light do you mean weak, and by heavy, strong?'

'Yes, I do; and I ask you whether you would give the same quantity of seed to both kinds, or to which you would give more?'

'Well, my principle is this: the stronger the wine, the more water I add; the stronger the bearer, the heavier the burden I put on his back; and if it is necessary to feed others, I should require the richest men to feed the greatest number. But tell me whether weak land, like draught animals, becomes stronger when you put more corn into it.'

'Ah, you're joking, Socrates,' he said, laughing, ' but allow me to tell you that, if after putting in the seed you plough it in again as soon as the blade appears when the land is obtaining plenty of nourishment from the sky, it makes food for the soil, and strengthens it like manure. If, on the other hand, you let the seed go on growing on the land until it is boiled, it's hard for weak land to yield much grain in the end. It's hard, you know, for a weak sow to rear a big litter of fine pigs.'

'Do you mean, Ischomachus, that the weaker the soil the less seed should be put into it?'

'Yes, of course, Socrates; and you agree when you say that your invariable custom is to make the burden light that is to be borne by the weak.'

'But the hoers, now, Ischomachus, why do you put them on the corn?'

'I presume you know that in winter there is a heavy rainfall?

'Of course.'

'Let us assume, then, that part of the corn is waterlogged and covered with mud, and some of the roots are exposed by flooding. And it often happens, you know, that in consequence of rain weeds spring up among the corn and choke it.'

'All these things are likely to happen.'

'Then don't you think that in such circumstances the corn needs prompt succor?'

'Certainly.'

'What should be done, do you think, to succor the part that is under the mud?'

'The soil should be lifted.'

'And the part that has its roots exposed?'

'It should be earthed up.'

'What if weeds are springing up, choking the corn and robbing it of its food, much as useless drones rob bees of the food they have laid in store by their industry?'

'The weeds must be cut, of course, just as the drones must be removed from the hive.'

'Don't you think, then, that we have good reason for putting on men to hoe?'

'No doubt; but I am reflecting, Ischomachus, on the advantage of bringing in an apt simile. For you roused my wrath against the weeds by mentioning the drones, much more than when you spoke of mere weeds.'

Book 18. 'However, I continued, 'after this comes reaping, I fancy. So give me any information you can with regard to that too.'

'Yes—unless I find that you know just what I do about that subject too. You know, then, that the corn must be cut.'

'I know that, naturally.'

'Are you for standing with your back to the wind when you cut corn, or facing it?'

'Not facing it, no! I think it is irritating both to the eyes and to the hands to reap with cornstalks and spikes blowing in your face.'

'And would you cut near the top or close to the ground ? '

'If the stalk is short, I should cut low down, so that the straw may be more useful; but if it is long, I think it would be right to cut in the middle, in order that the threshers and winnowers may not spend needless trouble on what they don't want. I imagine that the stubble may be burnt with advantage to the land, or thrown on the manure heap to increase its bulk.'

'Do you notice, Socrates, that you stand convicted of knowing just what I know about reaping too?'

'Yes, it seems so; and I want to know besides whether I understand threshing as well.'

'Then you know this much, that draught animals are used in threshing?'

'Yes, of course I do; and that the term draught animals includes oxen, mules and horses.'

'Then do you not think that all the beasts know is how to trample on the corn as they are driven?'

'Why, what more should draught animals know?'

'And who sees that they tread out the right corn, and that the threshing is level, Socrates?

'The threshers, clearly. By continually turning the untrodden corn and throwing it under the animal's feet they will, of course, keep it level on the floor and take least time over the work.'

'So far, then, your knowledge is quite as good as mine.'

'Will not our next task be to clean the corn by winnowing, Ischomachus?'

'Yes, Socrates; and tell me, do you know that if you start on the windward side of the floor, you will find the husks carried right across the floor? '

'It must be so.'

'Is it not likely, then, that some will fall on the grain?'

'Yes, it is a long way for the husks to be blown, right over the grain to the empty part of the floor.'

'But what if you start winnowing against the wind? '

'Clearly the chaff will at once fall in the right place.'

'And as soon as you have cleaned the corn over one half of the floor, will you at once go on throwing up the rest of the chaff while the corn lies about just as it is, or will you first sweep the clean corn towards the edge, so as to occupy the smallest space?'

'Of course I shall first sweep the clean corn up, so that my chaff may be carried across into the empty space, and I may not have to throw up the same chaff twice.'

'Well, Socrates, it seems you are capable of teaching the quickest way of cleaning corn.'

'I really wasn't aware that I understood these things; and so I have been thinking for some time whether my knowledge extends to smelting gold, playing the flute, and painting pictures. For I have never been taught these things any more than I have been taught farming; but I have watched men working at these arts, just as I have watched them farming.'

'And didn't I tell you just now that farming is the noblest art for this among other reasons, because it is the easiest to learn?'

'Enough, Ischomaohus; I know. I understood about sowing, it seems, but I wasn't aware that I understood.'

Book 19. 'However, is the planting of fruit trees another branch of agriculture?' I continued.

'It is, indeed,' answered Ischomachus.

'Then how can I understand all about sowing, and yet know nothing of planting?'

'What, don't you understand it?'

'How can I, when I don't know what kind of soil to plant in, nor how deep a hole to dig, nor how broad, nor how much of the plant should be buried, nor how it must be set in the ground to grow best?'

'Come then, learn whatever you don't know. I am sure you have seen the sort of trenches they dig for plants.'

'Yes, often enough.'

' Did you ever see one more than three feet deep?

'No, of course not—nor more than two and a half.'

'Well, did you ever see one more than three feet broad?'

'Of course not, nor more than two feet.'

'Come then, answer this question too. Did you ever see one less than a foot deep?'

'Never less than a foot and a half, of course. For the plants would come out of the ground when it is stirred about them if they were put in so much too shallow.

'Then you know this well enough, Socrates, that the trenches are never more than two and a half feet deep, nor less than a foot and a half.'

'A thing so obvious as that can't escape one's eyes.'

'Again, can you distinguish between dry and wet ground by using your eyes?'

'Oh, I should think that the land round Lycabettus and any like it is an example of dry ground, and the low-lying land at Phalerum and any like it of wet.

'In which then would you dig the hole deep for your plant, in the dry or the wet ground?'

'In the dry, of course; because if you dug deep in the wet, you would come on water, and water would stop your planting.'

'I think you are quite right. Now suppose the holes are dug; have you ever noticed how the plants for each kind of soil should be put in?'

'Oh, yes.'

'Then assuming that you want them to grow as quickly as possible, do you think that if you put some prepared soil under them the cuttings will strike sooner through soft earth into the hard stuff, or through unbroken ground?'

'Clearly, they will form roots more quickly in prepared soil than in unbroken ground.'

'Then soil must be placed below the plant?'

'No doubt it must.'

'And if you set the whole cutting upright, pointing to the sky, do you think it would take root better, or would you lay part of it slanting under the soil that has been put below, so that it lies like a *gamma* upside down?'

'Of course I would; for then there would be more buds underground; and I notice that plants shoot from the buds above ground, so I suppose that the buds under the ground do just the same; and with many shoots forming underground, the plant will make strong and rapid growth, I suppose.

'Then it turns out that on these points too your opinion agrees with mine. But would you merely heap up the earth, or make it firm round the plant?'

'I should make it firm, of course; for if it were not firm, I feel sure that the rain would make mud of the loose earth, and the sun would dry it up from top to bottom; so the plants would run the risk of damping off through too much water, or withering from too much heat at the roots.'

'About vine planting then, Socrates, your views are again exactly the same as mine.'

'Does this method of planting apply to the fig too ?' I asked.

'Yes, and to all other fruit trees, I think; for in planting other trees why discard anything that gives good results with the vine?'

'But the olive—how shall we plant that, Ischomachus?'

'You know quite well, and are only trying to draw me out again. For I am sure you see that a deeper hole is dug for the olive (it is constantly being done on the roadside); you see also that all the growing shoots have stumps adhering to them; and you see that all the heads of the plants are coated with clay, and the part of the plant that is above ground is wrapped up.'

'Yes, I see all this.'

'You do! Then what is there in it that you don't understand? Is it that you don't know how to put the crocks on the top of the clay, Socrates?'

'Of course there is nothing in what you have said that I don't know, Ischomachus. But I am again set thinking what can have made me answer 'No' to the question you put to me a while ago, when you asked me briefly, Did I understand plant-ing? For I thought I should have nothing to say about the right method of planting. But now that you have undertaken to question me in particular, my answers, you tell me, agree exactly with the views of a farmer so famous for his skill as yourself! Can it be that questioning is a kind of teaching, Ischomachus? The fact is, I have just discovered the plan of your series of questions! You lead me by paths of knowledge familiar to me, point out things like what I know, and bring me to think that I really know things that I thought I had no knowledge of'.'

'Now suppose I questioned you about money,' said Ischomachus, 'whether it is good or bad, could I persuade you that you know how to distinguish good from false by test? And by putting questions about flute-players could I convince you that you understand flute-playing; and by means of questions about painters and other artists——'

'You might, since you have convinced me that I understand agriculture, though I know that I have never been taught this art.'

'No, it isn't so, Socrates. I told you a while ago that agriculture is such a humane, gentle art that you have but to see her and listen to her, and she at once makes you understand her. She herself gives you many lessons in the best way of treating her. For instance, the vine climbs the nearest tree, and so teaches you that she wants support. And when her clusters are yet tender, she spreads her leaves about them, and teaches you to shade the exposed parts from the sun's rays during that period. But when it is now time for her grapes to be sweetened by the sun, she sheds her leaves, teaching you to strip her and ripen her fruit. And thanks to her teeming fertility, she shows some mellow clusters while she carries others yet sour, so saying to you: Pluck my grapes as men pluck figs,— choose the luscious ones as they come.'

Book 20. And now I asked, 'How is it then, Ischomachus, if the operations of husbandry are so easy to learn and all alike know what must needs be done, that all have not the same fortune? How is it that some farmers live in abundance and have more than they want, while others cannot get the bare necessaries of life, and even run into debt?'

'Oh, I will tell you, Socrates. It is not knowledge nor want of knowledge on the part of farmers that causes one to thrive while another is needy. You won't hear a story like this running about: The estate has gone to ruin because the sower sowed unevenly, or because he didn't plant the rows straight, or because someone, not knowing the right soil for vines, planted them in barren ground, or because someone didn't know that it is well to prepare the fallow for sowing, or because someone didn't know that it is well to manure the land. No, you are much more likely to hear it said: The man gets no corn from his field because he takes no trouble to see that it is sown or manured. Or, The man has got no wine, for he takes no trouble to plant vines or to make his old stock bear. Or, The man has neither olives nor figs, because he doesn't take the trouble; he does nothing to get them. It is not the farmers reputed to have made some clever discovery in agriculture who differ in fortune from others: it is things of this sort that make all the difference, Socrates. This is true of generals also: there are some branches of strategy in which one is better or worse than another, not because he differs in intelligence, but in point of carefulness, undoubtedly. For the things that all generals know, and most privates, are done by some commanders and left undone by others. For example, they all know that when marching through an enemy's country, the right way is to march in the formation in which they will fight best, if need be. Well, knowing this, some observe the rule, others break it. All know that it is right to post sentries by day and night before the camp; but this too is a duty that some attend to, while others neglect it. Again, where will you find the man who does not know that, in marching through a defile, it is better to occupy the points of vantage first? Yet this measure of precaution too is duly taken by some and neglected by others. So, too, everyone will say that in agriculture there is nothing so good as manure, and their eyes tell them that nature produces it. All know exactly how it is produced, and it is easy to get any amount of it; and yet, while some take care to have it collected, others care nothing about it. Yet the rain is sent from heaven, and all the hollows become pools of water, and the earth yields herbage of every kind which must be cleared off the ground by the sower before sowing; and the rubbish he removes has but to be thrown into water, and time of itself will make what the soil likes. For every kind of vegetation, every kind of soil in stagnant water turns into manure.

'And again, all the ways of treating the soil when it is too wet for sowing or too salt for planting are familiar to all men—how the land is drained by ditches, how the salt is corrected by being mixed with saltless substances, liquid or dry. Yet these matters, again, do not always receive attention. Suppose a man to be wholly ignorant as to what the land can produce, and to be unable to see crop or tree on it, or to hear from anyone the truth about it, yet is it not far easier for any man to prove a parcel of land than to test a horse or to test a human being? For the land never plays tricks, but reveals frankly and truthfully what she can and what she cannot do. I think that just because she conceals nothing from our knowledge and understanding, the land is the surest tester of good and bad men. For the slothful cannot plead ignorance, as in other arts: land, as all men know, responds to good treatment. Husbandry is the clear accuser of the recreant soul. For no one persuades himself that man could live without bread; therefore if a man will not dig and knows no other profit-earning trade, he is clearly minded to live by stealing or robbery or begging—or he is an utter fool.

'Farming,' he added, 'may result in profit or in loss; it makes a great difference to the result, even when many labourers are employed, whether the farmer takes care that the men are working during the working hours or is careless about it. For one man in ten by working all the time may easily make a difference, and another by knocking off before the time; and, of course, if the men are allowed to be slack all the day long, the decrease in the work done may easily amount to one half of the whole. Just as two travellers on the road, both young and in good health, will differ so much in pace that one will cover two hundred furlongs to the other's hundred, because the one does what he set out to do, by going ahead, while the other is all for ease, now resting by a fountain or in the shade, now gazing at the view, now wooing the soft breeze; so in farm work there is a vast difference in effectiveness between the men who do the job they are put on to do and those who, instead of doing it, invent excuses for not working and are allowed to be slack. In fact, between good work and dishonest slothfulness there is as wide a difference as between actual work and actual idleness. Suppose the vines are being hoed to clear the ground of weeds: if the hoeing is so badly done that the weeds grow ranker and more abundant, how can you call that anything but idleness?'

'These, then, are the evils that crush estates far more than sheer lack of knowledge. For the outgoing expenses of the estate are not a penny less; but the work done is insufficient to show a profit on the expenditure; after that there's no need to wonder if the expected surplus is converted into a loss. On the other hand, to a careful man, who works strenuously at agriculture, no business gives quicker returns than farming. My father taught me that and proved it by his own practice. For he never allowed me to buy a piece of land that was well farmed; but pressed me to buy any that was uncultivated and unplanted owing to the owner's neglect or incapacity. Well farmed land, he would say, costs a large sum and can't be improved; and he held that where there is no room for improvement there is not much pleasure to be got from the land: landed estate and livestock must be continually coming on to give the fullest measure of satisfaction. Now nothing improves more than a farm that is being transformed from a wilderness into fruitful fields. I assure you, Socrates, that we have often added a hundredfold to the value of a farm. There is so much money in this idea, Socrates, and it is so easy to learn, that no sooner have you heard of it from me than you know as much as I do, and can go home and teach it to someone else, if you like. Moreover, my father did not get his knowledge of it at secondhand, nor did he discover it by much thought; but he would say that, thanks to his love of husbandry and hard work, he had coveted a farm of this sort in order that he might have something to do, and combine profit with pleasure. For I assure you, Socrates, no Athenian, I believe, had such a strong natural love of agriculture as my father.'

Now on hearing this I asked, ' Did your father keep all the farms that he cultivated, Ischomachus, or did he sell when he could get a good price?'

' He sold, of course,' answered Ischomachus, 'but, you see, owing to his industrious habits, he would promptly buy another that was out of cultivation.'

' You mean, Ischomachus, that your father really loved agriculture as intensely as merchants love corn. So deep is their love of corn that on receiving reports that it is abundant anywhere, merchants will voyage in quest of it: they will cross the Aegean, the Euxine, the Sicilian sea; and when they have got as much as possible, they carry it over the sea, and they actually stow it in the very ship in which they sail themselves. And when they want money, they don't throw the corn away anywhere at haphazard, but they carry it to the place where they hear that corn is most valued and the people prize it most highly, and deliver it to them there. Yes, your father's love of agriculture seems to be something like that.'

'You're joking, Socrates,' rejoined Ischomachus; ' but I hold that a man has a no less genuine love of building who sells his houses as soon as they are finished and proceeds to build others.'

' Of course; and I declare, Ischomachus, on my oath that I believe you, that all men naturally love whatever they think will bring them profit.'

Book 21. 'But I am pondering over the skill with which you have presented the whole argument in support of your proposition, Ischomachus. For you stated that husbandry is the easiest of all arts to learn, and after hearing all that you have said, I am quite convinced that this is so.'

'Of course it is,' cried Ischomachus; 'but I grant you, Socrates, that in respect of aptitude for command, which is common to all forms of business alike—agriculture, politics, estate-management, warfare—in that respect the intelligence shown by different classes of men varies greatly. For example, on a man-of-war, when the ship is on the high seas and the rowers must toil all day to reach port, some boatswains can say and do the right thing to sharpen the men's spirits and make them work with a will, while others are so unintelligent that it takes them more than twice the time to finish the same voyage. Here they land bathed in sweat, with mutual congratulations, boatswain and seamen.

There they arrive with a dry skin; they hate their master and he hates them. Generals, too, differ from one another in this respect. For some make their men unwilling to work and to take risks, disinclined and unwilling to obey, except under compulsion, and actually proud of defying their commander: aye, and they cause them to have no sense of dishonor when something disgraceful occurs. Contrast the genius, the brave and scientific leader: let him take over the command of these same troops, or of others if you like. What effect has he on them? They are ashamed to do a disgraceful act, think it better to obey, and take a pride in obedience, working cheerfully, every man and all together, when it is necessary to work. Just as a love of work may spring up in the mind of a private soldier here and there, so a whole army under the influence of a good leader is inspired with love of work and ambition to distinguish itself under the commander's eye. Let this be the feeling of the rank and file for their commander; and I tell you, he is the strong leader, he, and not the sturdiest soldier, not the best with bow and javelin, not the man who rides the best horse and is foremost in facing danger, not the ideal of knight, but he who can make his soldiers feel that they are bound to follow him through fire and in any adventure. Him you may justly call high-minded who has many followers of like mind; and with reason may he be said to march with a strong arm whose will many an arm is ready to serve; and truly great is he who can do great deeds by his will rather than his strength.

'So too in private industries, the man in authority —bailiff or manager—who can make the workers keen, industrious and persevering—he is the man who gives a lift to the business and swells the surplus. But, Socrates, if the appearance of the master in the field, of the man who has the fullest power to punish the bad and reward the strenuous workmen, makes no striking impression on the men at work, I for one cannot envy him. But if at sight of him they bestir themselves, and a spirit of determination and rivalry and eagerness to excel falls on every workman, then I should say: this man has a touch of the kingly nature in him. And this, in my judgment, is the greatest thing in every operation that makes any demand on the labor of men, and therefore in agriculture. Mind you, I do not go so far as to say that this can be learnt at sight or at a single hearing. On the contrary, to acquire these powers a man needs education; he must be possessed of great natural gifts; above all, he must be a genius. For I reckon this gift is not altogether human, but divine—this power to win willing obedience: it is manifestly a gift of the gods to the true votaries of prudence. Despotic rule over unwilling subjects they give, I fancy, to those whom they judge worthy to live the life of Tantalus, of whom it is said that in hell he spends eternity, dreading a second death.'

THUCYDIDES, HISTORY OF THE PELOPONNESIAN WAR: BOOK VII. CHAPTER XXIII.

Demise of the Athenians: Rout at the Assinarus (description of military debacle)

As soon as it was day Nicias put his army in motion, pressed, as before, by the Syracusans and their allies pelted from every side by their missiles, and struck down by their javalins. The Athenians pushed on for the Assinarus, impelled by the attacks made upon them from every side by a numerous cavalry and the swarm of other arms, fancying that they should breathe more freely if once across the river, and driven on also by their exhaustion and craving for water. Once there they rushed in, and all order was at an end, each man wanting to cross first, and the attacks of the enemy making it difficult to cross at all; forced to huddle together, they fell against and trod down one another, some dying immediately upon the javelins, others getting entangled together and stumbling over the articles of baggage, without being able to rise again. Meanwhile the opposite bank, which was steep, was lined by the Syracusans, who showered missiles down upon the Athenians, most of them drinking greedily and heaped together in disorder in the hollow bed of the river. The Peloponnesians also came down and butchered them, especially those in the water, which was thus immediately spoiled, but which they went on drinking just the same, mud and all, bloody as it was, most even fighting to have it.

At last, when many dead now lay piled one upon another in the stream, and part of the army had been destroyed at the river, and the few that escaped from thence cut off by the cavalry, Nicias surrendered himself to Gylippus, whom he trusted more than he did the Syracusans, and told him and the Lacedaemonians to do what they liked with him, but to stop the slaughter of the soldiers. Gylippus, after this, immediately gave orders to make prisoners; upon which the rest were brought together alive, except a large number secreted by the soldiery, and a party was sent in pursuit of the three hundred who had got through the guard during the night, and who were now taken with the rest. The number of the enemy collected as public property was not considerable; but that secreted was very large, and all Sicily was filled with them, no convention having been made in their case as for those taken with Demosthenes. Besides this, a large portion were killed outright, the carnage being very great, and not exceeded by any in this Sicilian war. In the numerous other encounters upon the march, not a few also had fallen. Nevertheless many escaped, some at the moment, others served as slaves, and then ran away subsequently. These found refuge at Catana.

The Syracusans and their allies now mustered and took up the spoils and as many prisoners as they could, and went back to the city. The rest of their Athenian and allied captives were deposited in the quarries, this seeming the safest way of keeping them; but Nicias and Demosthenes were butchered, against the will of Gylippus, who thought that it would be the crown of his triumph if he could take the enemy's generals to Lacedaemon. One of them, as it happened, Demosthenes, was one of her greatest enemies, on account of the affair of the island of Pylos; while the other, Nicias, was for the same reasons one of her greatest friends, owing to his exertions to procure the release of the prisoners by persuading the Athenians to make peace. For these reasons the Lacedaemonians felt kindly towards him; and it was in this that Nicias himself mainly confided when he surrendered to Gylippus. But some of the Syracusans who had been in correspondence with him were afraid, it was said, of his being put to the torture and troubling their success by his revelations; others, especially the Corinthians, of his escaping, as he was wealthy, by means of bribes, and living to do them further mischief; and these persuaded the allies and put him to death. This or the like was the cause of the death of a man who, of all the Hellenes in my time, least deserved such a fate, seeing that the whole course of his life had been regulated with strict attention to virtue.

The prisoners in the quarries were at first hardly treated by the Syracusans. Crowded in a narrow hole, without any roof to cover them, the heat of the sun and the stifling closeness of the air tormented them during the day, and then the nights, which came on autumnal and chilly, made them ill by the violence of the change; besides, as they had to do everything in the same place for want of room, and the bodies of those who died of their wounds or from the variation in the temperature, or from similar causes, were left heaped together one upon another, intolerable stenches arose; while hunger and thirst never ceased to afflict them, each man during eight months having only half a pint of water and a pint of corn given him daily. In short, no single suffering to be apprehended by men thrust into such a place was spared them. For some seventy days they thus lived all together, after which all, except the Athenians and any Siceliots or Italiots who had joined in the expedition, were sold. The total number of prisoners taken it would be difficult to state exactly, but it could not have been less than seven thousand.

This was the greatest Hellenic achievement of any in this war, or, in my opinion, in Hellenic history; at once most glorious to the victors, and most calamitous to the conquered. They were beaten at all points and altogether; all that they suffered was great; they were destroyed, as the saying is, with a total destruction, their fleet, their army-- everything was destroyed, and few out of many returned home.

Appendix D: *Ober,* Civil War and Political Thought in Classical Greece

Josiah Ober, Princeton University

The Athenian situation in 403 B.C. was set up by a long and hard external war between Athens and Sparta. But it was also set up by a civil war between Athenians. The Greeks called civil war <u>stasis</u>. In order to understand the motives of individual Athenians, and the threats and opportunities that confronted the city in 403, it is necessary to get a proper understanding of the potential catastrophe that the Athenians confronted in 403: we need to see how bad a <u>stasis</u> really could be. Many classical Athenian writers were deeply concerned with <u>stasis</u> and attempted not only to offer an accurate description of civil conflict, but to understand its social roots, the relationship between civil conflict and external war, and the abnormal social psychology that accompanied extended periods of conflict. One of these writers was Thucydides, whose *History of the Peloponnesian War* is perhaps the first scholarly work of history. Thucydides presented the civil war that broke out in the island state of Corcyra in 427 B.C. as a sort of case study of the horrors of <u>stasis.</u>

BACKGROUND: THUCYDIDES' DESCRIPTION OF CIVIL WAR IN CORCYRA

In just a few pages of terse prose Thucydides describes the unraveling of the great city-state, Corcyra, in a traumatic <u>stasis</u>. The conflict was exacerbated by the Peloponnesian War, the protracted struggle between imperial Athens and Sparta's Peloponnesian League that had begun in 431 B.C. Corcyra had made a defensive alliance with Athens after losing a naval battle to Sparta's ally Corinth. After the alliance was struck, certain Corcyraeans who had been taken prisoner by the Corinthians, and had come to favor the Peloponnesian side, returned to Corcyra and began to agitate against the Athenian alliance. When the former POWs were unable to pass the requisite legislation in the Corcyraean assembly, they tried another tack, indicting Peithias, a Corcyraean Councilor and the leader of the pro-Athenian Corcyraean democrats, on a legal charge of treason.

Constitutional politics enters the story at this point: the conflict over foreign alliances was intimately connected to a conflict between political factions within Corcyra advocating rival political programs, that is, Democrats striving for a constitution that would make all native male Corcyraeans (including laborers and small farmers) into full citizens, versus oligarchs who sought the domination of a few relatively wealthy property-holders. Peithias' oligarchic opponents failed in their legal attack. Peithias was acquitted, and he retaliated with a ploy that underlines the role of class antagonism in Corinthian politics: he charged five of his wealthiest opponents with an act of impiety for illegally cutting saplings, for use as vine-stakes on their private estates, from a tract of state-owned sacred land. Upon being convicted and charged enormous fines for their act of impiety, Peithias' opponents fled to a temple, claiming sanctuary. Unable to pay their fines despite their great wealth, they were stripped of their ordinary legal protections as citizens, but as suppliants in a temple they were under the protection of the gods. The men in the temple soon learned that Peithias intended to enforce the full penalty and furthermore that he sought to extend the scope of the Athenian alliance. They rallied their supporters, burst into the Councilhouse, and murdered Peithias along with 60 other Councilors. The stasis had begun in earnest and the stakes were high: the victors would decide what alliances Corcyra would make (Athenian or Peloponnesian), what constitution Corcyra would have (democracy or oligarchy), and what classes of Corcyraeans would enjoy the privileges of citizenship (all native males, or only the rich). Somewhat similar considerations about alliances and constitutional arrangements, pertained in Athens in 403, in the aftermath of the return to power of the democrats.

Peithias' oligarchic opponents called a public assembly and forced through a decree repudiating the Athenian alliance. Next, with the help of the crew of a Corinthian ship, they launched an armed attack on the surviving democrats. The latter took up defensive positions on and around Corcyra's acropolis. Both sides sought assistance from the unfree population, but it was the democrats who successfully recruited the bulk of Corcyra's rural slaves with a promise of freedom (note that slaves also aided the democratic side in the Athenian stasis). Meanwhile, a small Athenian naval force arrived at Corcyra. Its commander sought to quell the violence, but he was soon confronted by a large Corinthian fleet. The Corinthian ships were forced to retreat in turn upon the arrival of a yet larger Athenian force.

The arrival and departure of outside military forces (Athenian and Peloponnesian) further fueled Corcyra's internal fighting, which waxed ever more destructive. To forestall a democratic counter-attack, the oligarchs set fire to the buildings around the agora, which resulted in massive loss of property and risked a general conflagration. The fighting soon drew in unexpected sectors of the population. Thucydides highlights these distortions of normal Greek society: "The women also joined in the fighting with great daring, hurling down tiles from the rooftops and standing up to the din of battle with a courage beyond their sex" (3.74). The stasis climaxed in a paroxysm of killing during which the now-dominant democrats cornered and slaughtered their less numerous opponents: "There was death in every shape and form. And, as usually happens in such situations, people went to every extreme and beyond it. There were fathers who killed their sons; men were dragged from the temples and butchered on the very altars; some were actually walled up in the temple of Dionysus and died there" (Thuc. 3.81). This was exactly what many people in Athens expected would happen upon the victory of the democrats.

Thucydides goes on to say that the stasis in Corcyra was simply the first, and not the worst, of a wave of civil conflicts that shattered many Greek poleis during the long Peloponnesian War. Moreover, the drawn-out international war, in Thucydides' view, worsened internal conflicts: "In times of peace and prosperity cities and individuals alike follow higher standards... but war is a stern teacher; in depriving people of the power of easily satisfying their daily needs, it brings most people's minds down to the level of their actual circumstances" (3.82). The two sides at Corcyra were defined by their preference of great-power alliance (Athens vs. Sparta), by their support for a specific system of government (democracy vs. oligarchy), and by their economic class (poor vs. rich). But the original issues became blurred as the violence escalated. Thucydides points out that each side advertised the justice of its own position by means of attractive slogans: "On the one side, political equality for the masses, and on the other side the safe and sound government of the aristocracy." But behind these slogans Thucydides detected a brutal lust for self-aggrandizement: " They were deterred neither by the claims of justice nor by the interests of the state; their one standard was the pleasure of their own side at that particular moment and so... they were always willing to satisfy the hatreds of the hour" (3.82).

In thinking about how different sorts of people would be likely to act in Athens in 403, it is important to note that although Thucydides' Corcyra narrative concentrates on the doings of citizen men of military age, it also shows how violent internal struggles drew in women and slaves, persons classical Greeks ordinarily expected to be neither citizens nor warriors: The civil conflict also became deeply entangled with aspects of the polis life that might not, at first glance, seem political: law, religion, and economic interests. Thucydides points out to his reader how, under the conditions of civil war, the various category distinctions that sustained the polis in more peaceful times -- rich and poor, free and slave, male and female, religious and secular, just and expedient, public and private -- were at once proclaimed with special vehemence in words and suffered utter collapse in practice. Strangely, it was only when these ordinary social rules were suspended and political consensus shattered that the unitary polis was revealed in all its diversity: the interests of the citizen men were seen to be inextricably bound up with those of women and slaves; religion, politics, and law appeared as part of a single system, driven by some deeper impulse. The big question for the Athenians in 403 would be: "Can we and should we return to 'normalcy' -- and if so just what will a return to 'normalcy' actually mean for each of us"?

Thucydides' account suggests that the driving passion behind the struggle was political: who would have the power to establish the rules by which society would be structured and who would have a share in its governance? The ultimate issue in the Corcyraean conflict, as in the civil conflict in Athens, was the composition of the citizen body: the key to the question "Who will rule?" lay in deciding "Who will be allowed to be an active, participatory citizen?" Who would gain the right to stand forth publicly and proudly, at the center of society, as its rightful masters? Would it be the heads of a few wealthy and well-born families? Or should the privileges and duties of citizenship be extended to a wider segment of the citizen body? And if so, how much wider? To all landowners? To all soldiers? To craftsmen and traders? To landless day laborers? To all those who aided the winning side in the conflict? At what point would the expansion of the citizenship threaten the basic categories and distinctions on which Greek culture was based -- and so foster more revolution? What were the ultimate social boundaries -- gender? residence? birthright? ethnicity? -- beyond which citizenship simply could not be imagined? As in Corcyra, these were key questions for Athenians in 403.

GREEK POLITICAL THOUGHT: WHAT ARE THE SOURCES OF CONFLICT? CAN IT BE PREVENTED?

The constitutional options facing Athens in 403 were democracy and oligarchy. Just what do these terms mean in the Greek context? In the course of describing another revolutionary situation, this time in late sixth-century Persia, Thucydides' elder contemporary, Herodotus, identified these two options, as well as monarchy, as the three governmental options taken seriously by the classical Greeks. Herodotus reports that a small group of Persian nobles, having violently overthrown a usurper-junta, sat down to discuss how the Persians ought to be governed. One of them advocated the rule of a privileged few (oligarchy), another the democratic rule of the many (democracy, here called isonomia -- literally "equality in respect to legal standing"), and a third the monarchical rule of a single individual. Not surprisingly perhaps, in light of actual Persian political history, Herodotus' Persians ultimately decide that monarchy is best for them. Yet despite the fact that tyranny remained common among the Sicilian Greeks, by the fifth century B.C. the primary governmental options for mainland city-states of Greece were various forms of oligarchy and democracy. And this meant in principle, a choice between the rule of some segment of the propertied classes or the rule of the entire native adult male population (the demos). It is important to come to grips with the kind of reasoned arguments made by both oligarchs and democrats in favor of their own preferred form of government. Although Greek politics included a lot of name calling, it was also based on matters of real political principle.

As Thucydides' depiction of revolutionary Corcyra suggests, deciding whether political claims based on property-holding were more or less legitimate than claims based on regional residence and native ancestry was among the most intractable political problems faced by the classical Greeks. Just as Herodotus' Persian debate leads us to suppose, the Greek political debate tended to be carried out in negative terms. Since there were only two legitimate options, discrediting one's opponent was tantamount to establishing legitimacy for one's own political preference. The oligarchs pressed their claim by contending that democracy was the self-interested rule of a large faction defined only by lack of wealth -- that of the poor. In the view of the oligarchs the worst of these were wage laborers, dependent upon a paymaster: their characters were thought to be corrupted by the "slavish" conditions of their employment. According to the oligarchs, because laborers were not truly free men, they were incapable of making independent judgments, and thus unworthy of participating in political deliberations. Meanwhile, democrats asserted that oligarchy meant the rule of the wealthy in their own material and excessively cosmopolitan interests. They claimed that those whose loyalty was to their goods could not be true patriots: oligarchs preferred the company of their fellow rich men in far-off places to their poorer fellows at home and they would willingly sacrifice their polis' independence in order to preserve their wealth. In sum, each side claimed that the other side ignored the common good of the polis as a state and as a society. Each claimed that the other was unjustly seeking to gain control over more than its fair share of the state's limited material and political resources.

Thucydides was both a historian and a political theorist. He was well aware of the long history of Greek intellectual debates over political legitimacy, as well as the equally long history of actual political conflicts. As Greek political writers moved between theory and practice, their careful observation of social practices stimulated the development of abstract political philosophy. Thucydides' account of events in Corcyra shows that he understood that economic interests were important in revolutionary activity, but he regarded conflicts between economic interests as an insufficient explanation of the actual course of events.

Like many other fifth-century intellectuals, especially the so-called Sophists (self-styled instructors in political wisdom, who flocked to Athens in the fifth century B.C.), Thucydides was fascinated by the relationship between existing social conventions and inherent human nature. A passage in the Corcyra narrative that may have been added to Thucydides' text by a later editor states baldly that it is precisely in periods of civil war that human nature itself was revealed most clearly, and in all is stark ugliness: "With the ordinary conventions of civil life thrown into confusion, human nature, always ready to offend even where laws exist, showed itself proudly in its true colors: as something incapable of controlling passion, insubordinate to the idea of justice, the enemy of anything superior to itself; for, if it had not been for the pernicious power of envy, men would not have exalted vengeance above innocence and profit above justice." (3.84).

Whether Thucydides wrote this passage or not, his historical-theoretical argument grimly suggests that when humans are confronted with a potentially unlimited capacity to self-aggrandize, the conventions of civilized life which ordinarily restrained vicious behavior will be swept away and under these conditions the state cannot survive. Civil conflict finds its logical end in the elimination of the free, independent state, which either destroys itself or leaves itself fatally exposed to external domination by the powerful. This, then, was the ultimate down side feared by almost all participants in the Athenian conflict of 403: the final collapse of civilized life and the end of Athens as a community. The problem of internal conflict within the polis was a key issue for classical Greeks, and thus it became a central concern of classical political thought. Given that civil war was regarded as an unmitigated evil, how could it be avoided? Or, if it could not be avoided altogether, could its effects be somehow softened? Must internal conflict lead to the death of the polis?

In The Republic, Thucydides' younger contemporary, and Socrates' student, the Athenian philosopher Plato offered a long, eloquent, and uncompromising answer to the problem of civil conflict and its relationship to human nature (as well as much else). Plato claimed that every existing polis was in fact at least two poleis unhappily coexisting in the same physical space. The rich and the poor were, in effect, cities unto themselves, with their own distinct cultures and values; hostilities between them were as inevitable as they were undesirable. For Plato, then, overt civil war was simply a hot phase in a chronic state of social conflict that would last as long as there could be any question or debate about who should be the rulers -- and (more radically) for as long as diversity of any sort pertained among the ruling classes.

Plato argued that the social divisions common to every existing polis reflected a profound psychological sickness, what we might today call a schizophrenic division within each individual human psyche. The Republic lays the framework for an idealized polis, Callipolis, based on the idea that true social harmony could only be achieved when persons whose souls were completely free from internal conflict were organized into a conflict-free polis and ruled by those possessing true wisdom. Every resident of Callipolis necessarily accepted the basic premise that each person is fit for only one task. For example, a shoemaker would limit his activity to shoemaking. He would not attend a political assembly in the morning and make shoes in the afternoon (as he might were he an Athenian citizen) because shoemaking and politics were distinct and mutually exclusive activities, to be undertaken by different persons. Plato's Callipolis was not an oligarchy, insofar as oligarchy meant the rule of a propertied class. In Callipolis it is the shoemaker's technical engagement in his craft, not his wealth, that precluded engagement in the political activity of ruling; whether he was a wealthy owner of a shoemaking factory or just scraping by with piecework was immaterial. Callipolis was divided into castes based on vocation, not wealth. A tiny cadre of philosophers served as the rulers. A more numerous caste of warriors, the Guardians, kept order and defended the state against its external enemies. And a mass of free but utterly apolitical producers of goods provided for the polis' material needs and were the society's only owners of private property.

Plato tells us little about the productive caste, but much of The Republic is devoted to the rules by which the philosopher-rulers and Guardians were to live their lives, to epistemological questions of absolute knowledge, and to the long and arduous educational program that would prepare them to fulfill their strictly defined political roles. The most remarkable aspect of the life of Callipolis' ruling elite is its radical egalitarianism and this egalitarianism crossed gender lines: male and female Guardians were to undertake essentially the same tasks, including military service. There was no private ownership of property among the Guardian class, no marriage, and no family life. Children were raised communally. The Guardians were as indistinguishable from one another as could be. None possessed anything, house, wife, child, apart from all others. The philosopher-rulers lived by the same social rules and primary upbringing as the Guardians, but they underwent many additional years of specialized philosophical training in order to achieve access to the knowledge that Plato felt was necessary to sustain the society according to its original and unchangeable founding premises.

Plato's ideas of what a proper social order might look like were radical, but not unique. Similar hyper-egalitarian ideas were parodied by the Athenian comedian, Aristophanes, in a play (The Assembly-women) presented in ca. 393 B.C., a decade after the Athenian conflict of 403 and a few years before Plato's masterpiece received its final form. In Aristophanes' comedy, the women of Athens, frustrated by the unpatriotic selfishness of their citizen-husbands, contrive to take over the government. They immediately institute a regime in which property is communalized and family life abolished. Even access to sexual pleasure is equalized via a measure that required the young and attractive to have sex with the old and ugly before being allowed access to their preferred partners. Aristophanes' witty play challenged its Athenian audience to think about the lack of fit between the political equality guaranteed by democracy, and pervasive distinctions based on class and gender. The women's egalitarian regime sought to remove the underlying causes of selfish self-aggrandizement and thereby eliminate the primary source of civil conflict.

A particularly pungent critique of this kind of utopianism came from Plato's own student, Aristotle, who argued that Plato's ideal polis was revealed as hopelessly impractical when viewed in the light of natural human impulses. Aristotle is a useful source of "common sense based" political philosophy. Like Thucydides, Aristotle assumed that accurate understanding of actual human nature, based on careful collection of historical evidence, was the key to genuinely useful political analysis. In the Politics, Aristotle argued that humans are by nature political animals -- which meant not only that they had a natural impulse to live sociably in groups, but also an impulse to contribute actively to the flourishing of the group by engaging in political life, ideally by "ruling and being ruled in turns." Although Aristotle notoriously claimed that children, women, and so-called "natural" slaves were psychologically unfit to be true political animals, this still left him with a large and socially diverse body of adult males as "natural" citizens. Confronting the tumultuous constitutional history of the Greek city-states, and Plato's utopian solution to the problem of civil strife, Aristotle asked whether there might be room for social diversity within a just and stable polis. Could fatal levels of social conflict be avoided without resorting to rigid castes, improbable social practices, and noble lies? Once again, these sorts of questions were centrally important to the Athenians in 403.

Aristotle assigned his students to collect comparative political-historical material from around the Greek world. The evidence suggested to him that there were some important similarities among many revolutions, but that civil conflict ultimately arose from a variety of causes. Like his predecessors, Aristotle recognized that conflicts between economic-class interests often motivated revolutionary activism, but, like Thucydides, he rejected class conflict as a single sufficient explanation: "For just as in war the crossing of ditches, even if they are very small, splits apart the ranks, so every difference [between people's circumstances and characters], it appears, makes for a factional split. The greatest split is perhaps that between virtue and depravity, then there is that between wealth and poverty, and so on, with others in varying degrees" (Politics 1303b12-16). But beneath all destructive conflict lay the tendency for men to form interest groups based on the distinctions among them, for those groups to seek to gain more than their fair share of available goods, and their willingness to resort to violence in that undertaking. It is the formation of groups based on political principles and perceived interests that lies at the center of any "solution" that the Athenians of 403 might come to -- and was the key to victory for any given faction.

DEMOCRACY AT ATHENS AND ITS CRITICS

The best introduction to the political tradition critical of Athenian democracy is a short tract written a generation before 403 B.C., in the third quarter of the fifth century (ca. 440-427). The arguments in this pamphlet, and other fifth century B.C. intellectual trends, will help to explain the kinds of arguments that were in the air in 403. Its anonymous author, dubbed by modern scholars "The Old Oligarch," assumes the persona of an anti-democratic Athenian instructing a sympathetic foreign friend about the peculiarities of his native polis. The Old Oligarch seeks to explain how and why the consistently self-interested behavior of "the democratic multitude" has led Athens to a position of international strength. He ironically praises the Athenian demos -- which he identifies as a faction consisting of "the poor and many" -- for its single-minded and selfish pursuit of its own advantage, and implicitly urges his pro-oligarchic readers, the "few who are good," to smarten up and behave likewise. The Old Oligarch himself seems to regard successful revolution as next to impossible, given the democracy's capacity to deceive, coerce, or overawe its internal and external enemies. But his conviction that democrats and oligarchs alike would always seek to promote their own factional interests, rather than the good of the state, sets the scene for destructive civil conflicts like Corcyra's -- or like Athens in 404 B.C.

At least some of the Old Oligarch's fifth-century contemporaries agreed that the democracy should be done away with, and they were less pessimistic than he about their chances for success. The two generations after the popular Athenian revolution of 508/7 had witnessed the extension and elaboration of democratic institutions, and the concomitant development of the political consciousness of the Athenian people. In 462 the conservative politician Cimon had sought to strengthen Athens' ties with oligarchic Sparta, but his plans backfired when the Spartans haughtily turned away Athenian military aid in suppressing a revolt by Sparta's subject class, the *Helots* of Messenia (see below). Cimon's political star plummeted. Immediately following the debacle, a democratic politician named Ephialtes proposed a legislative initiative that was passed in the Assembly: the Areopagus council, a governing body comprised of leading aristocrats, was stripped of certain of its powers of constitutional oversight. Ephialtes was subsequently murdered, but his young colleague Pericles was already rising to prominence as a new model democratic leader -- a master orator, skillful general, and innovative policy-maker. Pericles publicly rejected the old style aristocratic politics, which had focused on networking among small bands of trusted friends (the political clubs know as hetairiai). Instead of doing politics in the backroom forum of the private drinking party, Pericles developed a loyal, if informal, mass constituency of ordinary Athenians through speechmaking in the Assembly. Until the end of the fifth-century the tight little world of the political clubs would be regarded with suspicion by non-elite Athenians, as the primary site of anti-democratic plotting.

Through the middle decades of the fifth century the possibility of changing Athenian government to some form of oligarchy continued to fuel the rivalries among Athens' politicians. In the best known of these confrontations Thucydides, the son of Melesias (probably a relative of the historian, whose father was Olorus), sought to challenge Pericles in the key public forum of the Assembly. Thucydides arranged for wealthy and anti-democratic citizens to sit together, heckle their political opponents, and vote as block in the Assembly. It was too little, too late: A series of bold legislative initiatives had left the Athenian demos in full control of the governmental apparatus, and the demos was in no mood to be dictated to by the wealthy few. In 443 the Assembly elected to hold an ostracism -- a remarkable institution in which the Athenian citizens voted with inscribed potsherds to determine which prominent individual among them should be sent into exile for ten years. The institution itself, which dates back to the foundation of popular rule at Athens, is an eloquent statement about the scope of authority claimed by the demos -- in this case to expel a citizen (although no more than one each year) who was guilty of nothing other than political notoriety. In 443 it was the son of Melesias who "won" the unpopularity contest; his departure from the political scene left the pro-oligarchic Athenians leaderless. The politician Thucydides' failed attempt to challenge democracy in public provides the context for the Old Oligarch's negative assessment of democracy's morality and his pessimism about its probable longevity. After the ostracism of Thucydides the oligarchic movement went underground and some of the political clubs became centers of revolutionary agitation.

Meanwhile, critical intellectuals continued to challenge the implicit premises of the democratic regime. Borrowing the Sophists' sharp distinction between nature (physis) and custom (nomos), critics of democracy claimed that the rule of the people was a flimsy social construct, both perverse and artificial in that its laws and customary practices were contrary to basic laws of nature. In a true state of nature, these critics argued, a few strong and intrinsically excellent men would rule a herd of inferior persons. They would use that herd for their own instrumental purposes, just as a shepherd sheers or slaughters his sheep as it happens to suit his own pleasures. Democracy, they claimed, only continued to exist because the inferior herd, rightly fearing the capacity of the elite few, had managed to trick and coerce them into accepting an understanding of social justice based on a false notion of equality: the assumption that each citizen, despite his individual attainments or lack of them, was of equal political worth, and thereby worthy of an equal vote in the citizen Assembly. Anti-democratic intellectuals opposed this "arithmetical" -- one man one vote -- conception of equality with a contrary view of "natural" equality -- the idea that each man's rightful share of social and political goods should be determined by his strength and inherent excellence. On this reasoning, democracy was unnatural and oligarchy, the rule of the strong and excellent (and, it hardly need be said, the wealthy) was what nature intended.

But other fifth-century intellectuals provided arguments in support of democracy. The Sophist Protagoras of Abdera, for example, taught that political capacity (unlike physical strength or even intrinsic intelligence) was not in fact the monopoly of a few, but was distributed generally among the human race (or at least among adult, male Greeks). Protagoras developed a form of human-centered pragmatism that rejected the notion that there was any metaphysical truth to be known about matters such as justice or truth. If there was no final "god-approved" or even "natural" social order, then existing customs did constitute all the social reality that was accessible to humans -- and consequently their customs should be taken seriously. If, in Protagoras' most famous slogan, "man is the measure of all things," then human customs have all the force of natural laws. If democracy worked well in practice by producing various material and psychic goods for the citizens -- as, in mid-fifth century Athens it certainly did -- then this was evidence that the political capacity that was widely distributed among humans was indeed being aggregated efficiently. The key to Athens' material success in the fifth century was its empire, and the empire was secured by a large and efficient *trireme* navy. The model of the *trireme*, in which scores of ordinary men worked towards a common end by aggregating their individually puny strength, thereby transforming a mass of timber into a devastatingly effective naval weapon, was a fitting metaphor for Protagoras' understanding of democracy. And, as the Old Oligarch ruefully recognized, the experience of rowing in the fleet decidedly reinforced the lower class Athenian citizens' sense of their own worth and their collective power.

POLITICAL CONFLICT ON STAGE

Serious discussion of political matters was not restricted to intellectual circles. Athenian dramatists reconfigured the ideas of the Sophists and other fifth-century thinkers, often in familiar mythic terms, and presented them annually to huge audiences in the Theater of Dionysus. All Athenian dramatic productions were subsidized by the democratic state, and state officials were responsible for choosing each year's plays. Although Athenian tragedy took account of a great deal more than political theory and practice, there was obviously a close relationship between the civic arena and the tragic stage. Three examples of such plays, Aeschylus' Eumenides, Sophocles Antigone and Euripides' Ion explore how human nature related to divine will, man-made laws, and traditional custom, and what all this meant for the governance of the polis. Briefly reviewing these three dramatic plots clarifies the ways in which large audiences of ordinary citizens engaged with political-philosophical problems. Moreover, since drama served as a common education for Athenians of all classes, drama offers another treasury of arguments useful for advancing a variety of positions.

The Eumenides begins with Orestes, a prince of Argos, seeking sanctuary in Athens. Orestes had murdered his mother to avenge his father. He is pursued by the Furies, grotesque female divinities charged with the punishment of those who have shed the blood of kinfolk. Athens' tutelary goddess, Athena, refuses to grant Orestes sanctuary on her own authority; instead she creates the Areopagus Council as a citizen's court, and bids the Councilors to decide the justice of the matter. Orestes and the Furies present their cases, the jury is polled, and the decision goes in favor of Orestes (although only after Athena herself has cast the tie-breaking vote). Orestes is grateful, and offers a permanent alliance with Argos. The Furies, however, are angry and threaten revenge: the outbreak of a dreadful stasis among the Athenians. But they are eventually persuaded by Athena's skillful rhetoric (and veiled threats) to take up residence in Athens, and to turn their threat of civil conflict into a blessing on Athena's land. Here, in a play produced shortly after the Assembly voted to reduce the extra-judicial powers of the Areopagus Council and some 30 years before the revolutionary crisis at Corcyra, we find a set of issues remarkably similar to those highlighted by Thucydides: the threat of stasis, bloodshed among kin, questions about religious authority and sanctuary, women acting like men, the ambiguous scope of law, foreign policy entanglements, and the problematic use of rhetoric. In this play, however, all turns out well in the end: the state is in effect founded rather than destroyed.

Sophocles' Antigone, set in Thebes, offers a darker picture of political conflict. Antigone has been forbidden by Thebes' King Creon the right to bury her dead brother, who had sought to overthrow Creon's rule by leading an armed force against Thebes. This sets up a conflict between the demands of traditional religious practice (kin must bury their dead) and the demands of political authority (the king's will is law). Antigone confronts Creon, who responds by asserting both the legitimacy of his authority and the impropriety of a woman speaking publicly about politics. Creon has his way, and Antigone is sentenced to die for her insubordinate refusal to obey the royal injunction. But Creon's house is shattered in the process; his own son chooses to perish with Antigone rather than live in the world defined by the unanswerable voice of his autocratic father. Whereas modern readers might immediately identify Creon as a villain and Antigone as a heroine, the Sophocles' play stubbornly refuses to demonize any of its characters: all act as they feel they must in order for the polis to survive. This stark confrontation between political authority and social norms simply cannot be happily resolved. Sophocles' Thebans are not yet fighting a civil war, but the Athenian audience recognized that a city so desperately divided against itself was ultimately doomed.

Euripides' Ion initially seems to concern specifically private matters: Creusa, Queen of Athens and (as she supposes) last surviving member of the original earth-born royal Athenian family, has come to Delphi with her non-Athenian husband, Xuthus, to consult the oracle about her infertility. As the audience quickly learns, however, Creusa had previously born a child after being raped by the god Apollo. That son, Ion, spirited away by his father from the cave in which he was born, now lives as a temple servant in Delphi, Apollo's holy seat. In the course of the play, Creusa and Xuthus come to believe that Ion was Xuthus' illegitimate son, and Xuthus eagerly prepares to adopt him as his heir. Creusa, personally affronted and disgusted at the thought of a non-Athenian gaining a place in the royal lineage, seeks to kill Ion. Her plan is foiled through divine intervention, she finally recognizes her son, and agrees to the adoption. Ion comes to Athens, where, as the audience is informed, he will father the entire race of the Ionians. This play brings to center stage the issue of citizenship, the myth of autochthony, and Athenian imperial ideology. Through its improbably happy ending, the Athenians can retain their special "earthborn" status and can claim ancestral authority over all Ionians -- convenient in that speakers of the Ionian dialect made up a large percentage of Athens' imperial subjects. As in the other tragedies considered here, politics, law, religion, bloodshed, foreign policy, and women's problematic role in the polis are very much to the fore.

The annual festival of Dionysus also featured a competition for comedic drama. The plays of Aristophanes, the only classical Athenian comic playwright whose complete plays still survive, are characterized by their biting social and political satire. In Aristophanes' comic Athens, politicians were invariably corrupt, citizens often venal and excessively absorbed with getting their dinners, jurors interested mostly in amusement and asserting their arbitrary power over hapless litigants, and women over fond of sex and wine. Yet as with tragedy, contemporary intellectual debates and the concern about the fragility of civic unity under the stress of external war were represented by Athenian comedians in dramatic form. Among Aristophanes' masterpieces is Lysistrata, a fantasy in which women from across the Greek world decide that they have had enough of the Peloponnesian War. Among other inconveniences, it keeps their husbands away from their beds and families. The women decide to end the war by a sex strike: upon returning home from the year's campaigning, husbands will find unwilling sex partners. To drive home their point the women seize the sacred Acropolis of Athens, where they are attacked by a body of aging Athenian *hoplites* in a comic restaging of the revolutionary uprising of 508/7. The play ends happily, as comedies must, with everyone going home to restored domestic bliss. Yet as in Thucydides on Corcyra, issues of religious violation and gender-role confusion are mixed up the problems of external war and civil strife.

Aristophanes' Clouds engages a somewhat different theme: the bizarre ideas and practices of "Socrates the Sophist." In this play, Socrates the philosopher was portrayed as crackpot natural scientist and teacher of useful verbal tricks that allow "a bad speech to defeat a good argument." Strepsiades, an ordinary Athenian who has foolishly married an aristocratic woman and is in debt due to the lavish tastes of their son, sends his son to Socrates in hopes that he will learn how to trick their creditors in the lawcourts. But the son learns instead to act according to "human nature" -- and to scorn the customs that allowed a father to discipline his son but restrained a son from raising a hand against his father. The play seems to suggest that sophistic doctrines about nature and custom were in fact undermining the paternal authority that was one of the bases of Athenian society. The inter-generational violence and the play's startling ending -- a desperate act of preventative arson in which Strepsiades' sets fire to Socrates "think-shop" with the hapless Sophist trapped inside -- again recall the deadly serious conflicts of Thucydides' Corcyra. Aristophanes' play offers insight into ways in which Socrates was viewed by his fellow Athenians - and thus helps to clarify the issues that might have led to his trial.

"Socrates the Sophist" was Aristophanes' creation, but he was clearly modeled on the real Socrates, who, by the time of the play's production in 423 B.C., was already known for unorthodox behavior and thought. As depicted by Plato in the Apology of Socrates, a free version of Socrates' self-defense at a real trial in 399 on charges of impiety and corrupting the youth, Socrates was also a pungent critic of Athenian ethical norms and political practices, including the widespread participation of ordinary citizens in government that was the defining feature of Athenian democracy. Socrates spent much of his time in the agora of Athens, discussing ethical questions with any Athenian willing to be subjected to his peculiarly probing conversational style. Socrates had little time for the Sophists' notions about nature and culture, and equally little time for popular assumptions about the inherent wisdom of the citizen masses. Socrates was not concerned with the theory of politics for its own sake, but he made analogies from animal nature that had profound implications for democratic governance. Socrates scornfully dismissed the popular idea that the decisions of "the many" -- as Assemblymen, Councilors, and jurors -- helped to educate the youth of the city by establishing appropriate norms of behavior and setting salutary examples. He suggested on the analogy of horse training that only a few persons (or maybe just one man) with a highly special set of talents and specialized knowledge, would be genuinely capable of improving the youth. Socrates' preferred analogy for his own role in the city was that of a gadfly, who lit upon his fellow citizens and sought to sting them into a healthy state of intellectual wakefulness. Socrates himself seems to have been uninterested in any revolutionary implications of his discourse, but they were not lost on some of the young men who enjoyed watching him dissect the flawed logic of his interlocutors. Some of them eventually became leaders of the Thirty Tyrants who seized control of Athens in 404 -- including the famous Critias.

SPARTAN OLIGARCHY: THE RISE AND FALL OF A POLITICAL IDEAL

Greeks like Critias, writers and would-be revolutionaries hostile to the idea of democracy, tended to look to Sparta as a model state: aristocratic in that it was ruled by the "virtuous few" and oligarchic in that a relative handful of rulers controlled most of the property. Thucydides the historian was impressed by Sparta's remarkable constitutional stability. He noted that, having survived a protracted stasis in their earlier history, the Spartans retained a single constitution for over 400 years. Despite some superficially democratic features, that constitution was extremely restrictive in that the great majority of native-born males resident in the Spartan home territory of Laconia were denied the chance of citizenship of any sort. Classical Spartan society was divided into three primary classes based in the first instance on birthright -- a warrior elite (the Spartiates), free inferiors (the Perioikoi = "Fringe-Dwellers"), and a large class of serf-like sharecroppers, tied to the soil and permanently subject to institutionalized oppression (the *Helots*). Moreover, the Spartans had, in the archaic era, annexed the adjacent territory of Messenia and forced the once-independent Messenians into *helot*age. Thucydides' comment about a long Spartan stasis refers to the fierce struggles which attended the creation of this colonial regime.

What other Greeks most admired about Sparta was the education and discipline of the Spartiate class. The Spartiates called themselves "the Similars." The goal of Spartiate culture was to forge a citizen body composed of men whose individual characteristics were submerged in a group identity based on uniformity, discipline, and military excellence. Young Spartiates were raised in a rigorous state-organized educational system wherein they learned to ignore physical discomfort and to depend on the members of their assigned unit. When a Spartiate reached manhood he was initiated into a social/military unit of Messmates. Any young man who was not accepted by one of the established Messes was permanently dropped from the ranks of the Spartiates. He became an "Inferior" and experienced what amounted to social death.

Each Spartiate held a state-assigned plot of land that was farmed by *Helots*. Although in fact a wealthy Spartiate might own considerable estates in addition to this state-plot, all Spartiates were expected to live according to a strict egalitarian code of behavior: clothing, food, houses -- all aspects of public and private life -- were to be "similar" to those of all other Spartiates. Each Spartiate kept a watchful eye on his compatriots, suspiciously anticipating any deviation from the established norms. In the famous Funeral Oration, Thucydides' Pericles pointedly contrasts Spartan regimentation with the relative liberality of Athenian society: "Just as our political life is free and open, so too is our day-to-day life in our relations to each other; we do not get into a state with our next-door neighbor if he enjoys himself in his own way..." It was exactly this freedom and openness that Sparta-loving Athenians like Critias despised.

On the battlefield, as at home, no Spartiate was to stand out in any way from his fellows: the discipline of the Spartan phalanx was the key to Sparta's capacity to dominate its neighbors in the Peloponnese. And those states in thrall to Sparta were expected to toe a strict constitutional line: Thucydides says that the Spartans saw to it that all member-states of the Peloponnesian League "were governed by oligarchies who would work in the Spartan interest" (1.19). This overtly politicized foreign policy helps to explain why civil conflicts during the Peloponnesian War were exacerbated by the conflict between the great powers: Everyone knew that a state joining the Peloponnesian League would necessarily adopt a Spartan-approved oligarchy. Aristocrats living in democratic cities sometimes aped superficial aspects of Spartan culture -- long hair, distinctive Laconian shoes and staffs, and Laconic speech mannerisms. These life-style choices signaled their hopes for Spartan help in imposing an oligarchic regime in which the poorer citizens would be disenfranchised.

Sparta, at least as it was imagined by oligarchic visionaries, bears some resemblance to Plato's Callipolis. But beneath the veneer of stability Sparta was permanently and literally at war with itself: Each year the Spartiates formally declared war upon the *Helot* population, a more-than-symbolic measure that allowed any Spartiate to treat any *Helot* as a foreign enemy. The Old Oligarch informs his reader that, quite shockingly in his view, in democratic Athens you were not allowed to strike slaves or foreigners at will. His apparent reference was to the Athenian law forbidding acts of deliberate outrage against any person, whether male or female, adult or child, free or slave. It was very different in Sparta, where individual *Helots* lived with the fear not merely of being struck, but murdered, by their masters. The <u>krypteia</u> -- a secret society staffed by young Spartiates -- transformed the sporadic violence against *Helots* into a ritual. Members of the <u>krypteia</u> would sneak about at night, selecting victims for assassination on the basis of any outstanding attribute, from extraordinary physical stature to overt evidence of ambition. From the perspective of the *Helot* population, at least, the Spartan <u>stasis</u> never ended; *Helots* lived out their lives in a society governed by the rule that the stronger will inflict their will upon the weak by whatever means they can contrive, where killing one's neighbors was an ordinary fact of life. This society recalls Thucydides' description of human behavior during a civil war. Spartan society was taken as a model by extreme oligarchs and remained one of the possible futures for Athens in 403.

CONCLUSIONS

In his depiction of the <u>stasis</u> at Corcyra, Thucydides had emphasized the link between physical violence and the corruption of ordinary language. He pointed out how fine names were attached to reprehensible deeds, and how rhetorical ability was employed to gain the selfish ends of personal revenge and private aggrandizement. The Greek experience of political conflicts between democrats and oligarchs in the fifth and fourth centuries demonstrated the potential brutality of Greek political life. Yet attempts to understand and transcend conflict also resulted in the flourishing of the sophisticated ethical and political thought that became the foundation of much of Western philosophy. Moreover, although oligarchy remained the preference of many elite Greeks, in the classical period and long thereafter, it was democracy that proved most resilient, most successful in moving beyond violent political conflicts to build a culture defined by productive political deliberation. It is that ideal that Athenian democrats in 403 clung to and that sustained them in the difficult conflict with their principled and self-interested opponents.

Appendix E: Recommended Reading

PRIMARY TEXTS

Note: some of these texts may be available online through the Perseus Project (www.perseus.tufts.edu)

Thucydides, *History of the Peloponnesian War* (Modern Library, or any edition)
   The war between Sparta and Athens, from 431 to 411 B.C.

Xenophon, *Hellenica,* or, *History of My Times* (Penguin or any edition)
   A continuation of Thucydides' history from 411 B.C. through the early decades of the 4th century.

Xenophon, *Recollections of Socrates and Socrates' Defense Before the Jury* (Bobbs-Merrill, or any edition of Xenophon's *Recollections/Memorabilia* and *Defense/Apology of Socrates*)
   An extended portrait and defense of Socrates in his dealings with the citizens of Athens; a brief account of Socrates on trial, which argues that Socrates intended his own execution—hence a more boastful and provocative Socrates, less philosophical and mysterious than the Socrates described by Plato.

Plato, *Apology of Socrates* (Cornell, or any edition)
   Socrates' defense before the jury, as recreated (or created) by Plato.

Plato, *Protagoras* (Chicago, or any edition)
   Especially the "great speech" of Protagoras [320d-328d], which purports to be a defense of democracy.

Aristotle, *Constitution of Athens* (Hafner, or any edition)
   Especially sections 34-69, which describe the installation and overthrow of the Thirty Tyrants and the constitution that reestablished democracy.

Aristotle, *Politics* (Chicago, or any edition)
   Especially III.9, which provides distributive justice arguments supporting (or critiquing) various regimes; III.11, which provides a qualified defense of democracy; and IV, V, VI which describe extreme and moderate versions of regimes, the vulnerabilities of various regimes to faction and civil war, and the mixed regime called polity.

Pseud-Xenophon ("The Old Oligarch"), *The Constitution of the Athenians* in *Aristotle and Xenophon on Democracy and Oligarchy*, J.M. Moore, ed. (California, or any edition that includes the "Old Oligarch's" constitution, so called)
> A cynical "appreciation" of the effectiveness of Athenian democracy in promoting the interests of the poor at the expense of the rich; useful for members of the Oligarchic faction especially.

Euripides, *The Trojan Women* (Chicago, or any edition)
> A tragedy of warfare and aggression contemporary with the Sicilian Expedition.

Aristophanes, *The Clouds* (Chicago, or any edition)
> A spoof on Socrates, which Plato claims *(Apology)* led to Socrates' trial and execution.

Aristophanes, *The Assemblywomen* (Chicago, or any edition)
> A spoof on Plato, in which women take over the Athenian Assembly and try to institute communism.

SECONDARY TEXTS

Allan Bloom, "Introduction" in *The Republic of Plato* (Basic Books)
> A penetrating analysis of the dialogue that manages to also to be accessible to first-time readers.

Christopher Carey, *Trials from Classical Athens* (Routledge)
> A detailed review of legal procedures and precedents.

Foustel de Coulanges, *The Ancient City* (Anchor Doubleday)
> A 19th century classic on the political institutions and social practices of the ancient world.

Robert Garland, *Daily Life of the Ancient Greeks* (Greenwood)
> A study of language and literacy, religion, work, slavery, and leisure; useful for indeterminates especially.

A.H.M. Jones, *Athenian Democracy* (Blackwell)
> Chapters on the workings of democracy and criticisms thereof; also on economics, social structure, population.

Donald Kagan, *On the Origins of War and the Preservation of Peace* (Anchor Doubleday)
>	An account of the Pentecontaetia, the 50 year period between the Persian War and the Peloponnesian War; plus studies of several other conflicts.

Wilmoore Kendall, "The People Versus Socrates Revisited," in *Contra Mundum* (Arlington House)
>	A defense of Athens in its prosecution of Socrates; especially useful for Radical Democrats.

Russel Meiggs, *The Athenian Empire* (Oxford)
>	A modern classic based on the tribute lists of ancient Athens.

Mark Munn, *The School of Athens: Athens in the Age of Socrates* (California)
>	An accessible narrative, extending from 510 to 395 B.C., which develops all of the issues of the game.

Josiah Ober, Mass *and Elite in Democratic Athens: Rhetoric, Ideology, and the Power of the People* (Princeton)
>	A study of the foundations of Athenian power.

Josiah Ober, *Political Dissent in Democratic Athens: Intellectual Critics of Popular Rule* (Princeton)
>	An account of how Athens defended itself in practice against its many theoretical critics.

Josiah Ober and Charles Hedrick, eds., *Demokratia: A Conversation on Democracies, Ancient and Modern* (Princeton)
>	Articles by current scholars using an ancient-modern comparative method.

Jennifer Tolbert Roberts, *Athens on Trial: The Antidemocratic Tradition in Western Thought* (Princeton)
>	Early chapters on the Athenian experiment and its critics, followed by chapters on the perception of Athens and Sparta over the centuries.

David Stockton, *The Classical Athenian Democracy*
>	An overview of Athenian democracy in its developed form